MAPLE SYRUP
C O O K B O O K

Ken Haedrich

Foreword by Marion Cunningham,
author of *The Fannie Farmer Cookbook*

Storey Publishing

*The mission of Storey Publishing is to serve our customers by
publishing practical information that encourages
personal independence in harmony with the environment.*

Edited by Dianne M. Cutillo
Art direction by Meredith Maker
Cover and text design by Erin Lincourt
Text production by Erin Lincourt and Jennifer Jepson Smith
Cover illustration © Warren Kimble
Interior illustrations by Ilona Sherratt
Recipe credits appear on page 133
Indexed by Nan Badgett/word•a•bil•i•ty

The information in this book is true and complete to the best of our knowledge. All recommendations are made without guarantee on the part of the author or Storey Publishing. The author and publisher disclaim any liability in connection with the use of this information. For additional information please contact Storey Publishing, 210 MASS MoCA Way, North Adams, MA 01247.

Storey books are available for special premium and promotional uses and for customized editions. For further information, please call 1-800-793-9396.

Maple Syrup Cookbook was first published as *The Maple Syrup Cookbook* in 1989. All of the information in the previous edition was reviewed and updated. This edition includes 32 new recipes and 39 new sidebars or tips.

Printed in the United States by McNaughton & Gunn, Inc.
20 19 18 17 16 15 14

Library of Congress Cataloging-in-Publication Data

Haedrich, Ken, 1954-
   Maple syrup cookbook : Over 100 recipes for breakfast, lunch & dinner / by
Ken Haedrich.— rev. ed.
      p. cm.
   Includes index.
   ISBN 978-1-58017-404-3 (alk. paper)
   1. Cookery (Maple sugar and syrup) 2. Maple syrup. I. Title.
TX767.M3 H35 2001
641.6'364—dc21

                                                                    2001034149

Contents

Foreword

In the traditions of the past, Ken Haedrich and I would be exchanging recipes over the back fence, as good friends and neighbors used to do. And judging from the recipes Ken has gathered here in *The Maple Syrup Cookbook,* a gratifying exchange it would have been.

Instead of over the back fence, Ken and I have had our kitchen talks over the phone for many years now. And we've exchanged our share of letters. In addition, I've followed his cooking column in *Country Journal* magazine, as well as the recipes and articles he has published elsewhere. Through it all, I've come to know Ken as a fine, American home cook who has great enthusiasm and a respect for simple, wholesome ingredients — an attitude that stands out clearly in his writing and recipes.

Recently, I visited Ken for the first time at his home in the quiet woods of New Hampshire, where he lives with his young family. When I sat down in Ken's kitchen and ate his good warm biscuits and pies — including several of the ones you'll find here — it was just the kind of homey visit with a friend that we all love.

With any luck, I'll be back to visit Ken soon. But in the meantime, if I can't eat his own good maple pies, cakes, cookies, and breakfasts, I can at least keep a copy of this book close by, to make them for myself.

It seems most appropriate that Ken, with his fondness for pure and simple ingredients, should write this maple syrup cookbook. Maple syrup is one of America's most delicious natural foods, and Ken has done a great job of giving us recipes that let the wonderful flavor of maple syrup come through.

— MARION CUNNINGHAM
AUTHOR OF *THE FANNIE FARMER COOKBOOK*
WRITTEN FOR THE 1989 EDITION

Preface

In the twelve years since this book was first published, many more people have discovered — or perhaps rediscovered — the liquid gold known as pure maple syrup. Foods featuring it are on menus, and not just breakfast menus, at restaurants from London to Beverly Hills and beyond. Today, maple syrup is sold in more than thirty countries, and production of it increased by 81 percent between 1990 and 2000.

More and more sugarmakers are opening up their operations to visitors to demonstrate their art, the process of converting watery sap to pure maple syrup, and to pass on a respect for the uniquely North American springtime ritual of sugaring. The producers, large and small, who have banded together into associations have strengthened their efforts to promote high-quality standards and the use of maple syrup.

Any of these things could have served as motivation for revision of this book. But, for me, the only reason I need is what motivated me to write a maple syrup cookbook in the first place: I love the stuff in a big way. As I said in the preface to the first edition, I love the flavor, the smell, and the color of pure maple syrup, a combination of sensual pleasures nobody has been able to capture with artificial ingredients. Real maple syrup is so special that its very presence in a dish or at a meal inspires awe and grabs attention. Serve it on pancakes, drizzle it on ice cream, marinate meat in it, or sweeten a cheesecake with it, and people take note, feel honored, as though a visiting dignitary had joined them for the meal. That's the magic quality I love about maple syrup.

Having lived and cooked in one capacity or another here in New Hampshire for the past twenty years I've had ample opportunity to experiment with pure maple syrup, to discover for myself where maple seems to work best in cooking. In addition, I've met a number of sugarmakers, professional cooks, and talented home cooks, many of whom are as passionate about maple syrup as I am. Not only has meeting these people deepened my admiration for maple — the natural result of getting to know the maple syrup producers themselves — but it has also influenced the way I use maple syrup in my cooking and steered me toward a repertoire of maple syrup recipes that I think reflects the ways cooks most enjoy using maple syrup in the kitchen.

That's what this cookbook is all about — enjoyable ways to use maple syrup in the kitchen. I've included many of my favorite recipes from the first book, and I've added new ones that reflect some of the more interesting ways maple is being used in the kitchen these days. I've also included cooking tips and maple lore that celebrate the spirit of maple and the tradition of sugarmaking. And, to honor the people from whom I've learned so much about maple, I introduce you to some sugarmakers, passionate souls whose love of maple makes them slaves for six weeks each spring to the sap that, miraculously, is transformed by boiling and tender loving care into liquid gold.

Here's hoping that all of the maple syrup recipes in this book, as well as any of your own adaptations they might inspire, give you and your loved ones as much pleasure as they have me and mine.

— Ken Haedrich

CHAPTER ONE

MAPLE: FROM TREE TO TABLE

Though it is widely believed that the Native Americans were experienced sugarmakers long before the white man arrived in North America, when and how they learned to make maple syrup is a mystery. A Native American legend has it that there was once a time when sap issued from the maple tree in a near-pure syrup form, something that a formidable god by the name of Ne-naw-Bozhoo decided to bring to a halt. Anticipating, no doubt correctly, that syrup thus had would be too easily taken for granted, he diluted it with water. Sugarmakers have been boiling the water out of sap ever since, in the pursuit of pure maple syrup.

The Native Americans are likely to have converted most of their maple syrup to maple sugar. Liquid storage vessels were few, and maple sugar was far easier to store and transport. They put their "Indian sugar" into specially made birch bark boxes known as *mokuks* and carried containers of it to market. Along with these larger blocks of maple sugar, which they sold or traded, the Native Americans made molded sugar candies. The molds were, as one observer noted, "cut from soft wood and greased before the sirup was put into them so that it could easily be taken out. These molds were in [the] shapes of various animals, also of men, and of the moon and stars, originality being sought."

Colonial Innovations

The arrival of early settlers in the Americas brought the white man's innovations to the sugarmaker's art. Foremost among these innovations were iron and copper kettles, which proved to be far less perishable than the wooden and clay troughs the Native Americans used for boiling sap. The white man realized that the Native American way of tapping maples — by cutting deep gashes into the bark — not only wasted sap but injured the trees. So he took to drilling tapholes with an auger.

The settlers further improved sap collection methods when they replaced the Native Americans' birch bark containers with more reliable ones fashioned from ash or basswood trees. The large trunk sections of these trees were cut to length, halved, and then hollowed out into crude troughs. Over time, these clumsy troughs were replaced by buckets and, finally, by hanging buckets, hung by metal spikes. The spikes were superseded by modern taps made to support the weight of the bucket or tubing.

The Native Americans boiled sap by dropping red-hot stones into wooden dugout troughs where the sap was held. And weather permitting, they would also remove water from sap by freezing instead of boiling. The water would rise to the top of the troughs and freeze, leaving unfrozen, concentrated sap below. The large cauldrons brought by the settlers were more efficient for boiling than the wooden troughs. In the kettle method of boiling, a large cauldron was suspended over a blazing fire, supported by a pole frame. Sometimes a series of kettles was used and the sugarmakers ladled the partially evaporated sap from one kettle to the next. In this way, syrup could be made on a continuous basis.

When you stop to consider the laborious nature of sugarmaking against the rigorous backdrop of pioneer life, you might wonder why the early settlers even made the effort. Were there no alternatives?

Maple Alternatives

There were alternative sweeteners, actually — honey being one. In fact, honeybees had been imported from Italy as early as 1630. But beekeepers were few in the colonies, and honey was relatively rare and would remain so for years to come.

Molasses, on the other hand, was abundant and soon began arriving from West Indian sugar plantations. (Sugar itself, of which molasses is a by-product, was still prohibitively expensive.) But molasses was a thorn in the side of the settlers, not just because of the high cost of transporting it from the coast by packhorse, but also because the molasses trade supported slavery in the most direct way. "Make your own sugar," advised the *Farmer's Almanac* in 1803, "and send not to the Indies for it. Feast not on the toil, pain and misery of the wretched."

Today, of course, maple products account for but a small fraction of the sweeteners used in the United States. However, just one hundred years ago — at least in the northeastern part of the country — maple ranked first among the sweeteners. Whereas a century ago 90 percent of the maple crop was converted to maple sugar, today only a small amount is, since most consumers buy maple primarily in syrup form for pancakes and waffles. Nonetheless, maple syrup, as more cooks are discovering every year, can indeed play a leading role in the modern kitchen.

Modern Maple Production

In some respects, very little about the process of making maple syrup has changed over time. Today, of course, sugarmakers have at their disposal a number of timesaving and laborsaving innovations, from plastic tubing to reverse-osmosis machines. But these inroads only hasten the transition from sap to syrup; in no way do they diminish maple's magic. The flavor, quality, and wholesome goodness of maple syrup have, if anything, improved over the years. And in an age when so many of our comestibles are nothing more than machine-made synthetics, maple syrup remains an oasis of purity, still made on the farm by men and women whose connection with the earth is part of their daily lives.

Maple syrup is produced in the northeastern and upper midwestern parts of the United States and in adjacent sections of Canada, covering a select area from Maine as far south as West Virginia and west to Minnesota. Though the range of *Acer saccarum* and *Acer nigrum*, the two principal sugar maples, extends beyond

"Frog Run"

Folk wisdom has it that when the frogs begin to sing, or spring peepers can be heard at night, spring is imminent. So, many sugarmakers call the last batch of sap that flows a "frog run."

this area, the unique combination of altitude, soil conditions, and weather patterns necessary for maple syrup production — freezing nights followed by warm, above-freezing days — does not. The Europeans, who have the trees but not the weather patterns, have tried without success to manufacture maple syrup on their own turf.

Maple sap is a clear liquid containing nutrients from the soil and organic substances manufactured by the leaves. It tastes somewhat sweet, with a sugar content averaging 2 to 3 percent, though the percentage can run as high as 6 percent, varying from tree to tree, from sugarbush to sugarbush, from one week to the next and from one year to the next. The sugar in the maple sap is synthesized by the leaves and stored in the tree as starch. This starch is the food of the plant, and in fall and spring, with the further action of sunlight, it is converted into sucrose and, in turn, to invert sugar in which the sucrose is broken down into glucose and fructose.

The Sugar Moon

Sugaring season begins as early as January and often extends well into April. The Native Americans, for whom this was a season of celebration, referred to this period as "the sugar moon." Sap does not flow in freezing weather, but as the warmer days of late winter return, the sap begins to move with vigor and sugarmakers set out their taps.

Tapholes are usually bored 2 to 2½ inches deep, with a ⁷⁄₁₆-inch bit. A bit and brace are sometimes used, but more common today is the automatic drill. Tapholes are drilled on a slight downward path to facilitate the flow of sap, and they are located anywhere from about 3 to 5 feet off the ground. Not just any sugar maple tree can, or should, be tapped. Those trees, for instance, yielding a sap with a sugar content of 1 percent are not considered economically worthwhile because of their low syrup yields and therefore are often culled.

Opinions vary, but conventional wisdom maintains that trees selected for tapping should have a minimum diameter of 12 inches, 4½ feet from the ground. As the diameter increases, so may the number of taps, at the rate of one tap for each 10-inch increase. Since tapping subjects the maple tree to stress, many experienced sugarmakers strongly recommend not exceeding 3 taps per tree, no matter how large the tree is.

Into every taphole a spout or *spile* is driven. All spouts have a tapered "shoulder" — the part that goes into the tree — in order to form a tight, leakproof seal with the bark and outer sapwood. Through the spout the sap flows, either into a sap bucket hung directly on the spout or into plastic tubing.

The standard sap bucket today is a 15-quart, galvanized metal container. It has a cover to keep out rain and assorted detritus. Sap buckets are emptied by hand and poured into a central, and usually portable, collection tank. Manual sap collection is a slow, labor-intensive activity and accounts, according to one source, for as much as one-third of the cost of syrup production.

The advent of plastic tubing has dramatically changed sap collection methods, and most large maple operations have made the switch from buckets to tubing. Tubing is not a perfect solution — squirrels nibble on it, moose trample through it, tree limbs fall on it, and careful cleaning is required. But it has eliminated much of the drudgery associated with manual sap collection. With tubing, one no longer needs to build roads or paths, often through inhospitable terrain, to gather sap. Tubing is light and easy to carry. And it allows for a continuous flow of sap to the sugarhouse or to roadside storage tanks.

Boiling Begins

Whether collected by bucket or fed by plastic tubing, all sap eventually finds its way to the sugarhouse to be boiled down to syrup. The typical modern sugarhouse is apt to have one or more large sap storage tanks, a wood-fired or oil-fired evaporator for boiling the sap, a finishing pan for completing the boiling, some type of filtering system, bulk storage barrels for storing the finished syrup, and a storage area for packaged syrup. Depending on the sophistication of

Maple Syrup: The Real Thing

Maple syrup is syrup made by the evaporation of maple sap or by the solution of maple sugar, and contains not more than approximately 33 to 35 percent water. That, by definition, is the real thing.

Then, of course, there's the imitation maple syrup, sometimes called pancake syrup, that is sold by several national food companies. Imitation maple syrup is mostly corn syrup and perhaps contains 2 or 3 percent of the real thing. For the purposes of this book, when we say *maple syrup* we're referring to pure, genuine, 100 percent maple syrup. If there is any question in your mind whether you are buying real syrup, read the packaging carefully.

Real maple syrup is indeed nothing more than 100 percent boiled sap, but other substances may find their way into the finished product. Generally, these substances are found only in trace amounts and are the result of standard maple syrup production practices. In all likelihood you'll never be aware of their presence. Rarely, very rarely, have producers been found to intentionally adulterate their maple syrup with corn syrup or other liquid sugars. If you suspect the syrup you've bought has been adulterated, contact the department of agriculture in the state where the syrup was purchased.

the operation, you may also find a reverse-osmosis machine, which removes up to 60 percent of the water content before the sap reaches the evaporator, and a specially equipped kitchen for the manufacture of maple sugar candies.

The backbone of the sugarhouse is the evaporator, essentially a large pan used for boiling water from the sap. Evaporators have come a long way since the wooden troughs used by the Native Americans. The modern evaporator was introduced in about 1900, and its advantages over its flat-bottomed predecessor are significant. Flues beneath the pan not only trap heat and increase fuel efficiency but also provide a greater heating surface, therefore increasing the rate of evaporation.

The typical evaporator is a two-pan affair supported by a heavy metal frame called an *arch.* From the storage tanks, the sap enters the sap or back pan, the larger of the two pans, where the boiling process begins. Great plumes of steam soon rise from the evaporator as the water is boiled out of the sap. Many evaporators have a

Easy Opening

Before returning maple syrup to the refrigerator, rinse the cap in hot water and wipe the top of the jug so the cap will be easier to remove the next time.

hood directly over the sap pan, enclosing a bank of pipes where incoming sap is preheated, which further speeds up the rate of evaporation.

Concentrated sap flows down the back pan and enters by a connecting pipe into the front or syrup pan, located over the firebox. The syrup pan is where the final or near-final stage of boiling takes place. As it gets closer and closer to finished density, the sap in the syrup pan moves through a series of baffles toward a draw-off valve. The purpose of the baffles is to guard against the constant intermixing of saps of different densities, so syrup can be drawn off on a continuous basis, instead of in one large batch. The result is higher-grade yields of syrup.

Experienced sugarmakers can tell by sight — judging by the color and the look of the bubbles in the syrup pan — when the syrup is ready to be drawn off. They'll dip a paddle or scoop into the pan, lift it up, and check to see whether the syrup "sheets" or "aprons" off the paddle in the fashion that indicates the syrup point has been reached. The precise tests for doneness, however, are based on readings from precision instruments.

MAPLE SYRUP GRADING AND USE

U.S.	CANADA	DESCRIPTION	RECOMMENDED USE
Grade A Light Amber	**No. 1 Extra Light**	Light and mild, this has what's known in the maple industry as a "maple bouquet," or a very delicate but clear maple flavor. It's usually made earlier in the season when the weather is colder and there's less chance of sap fermentation — one of the factors that contribute to dark, lower-grade syrup.	Maple candy, maple cream, cake icings, ice cream, delicate sweets.
Grade A Medium Amber	**No. 1 Light**	The most popular grade of table syrup, this is a bit darker and has a more pronounced maple flavor. Generally, this is made about midseason, after the weather starts to warm.	Used more as a table syrup, as on pancakes, waffles, and French toast, than for cooking and baking.
Grade A Dark Amber	**No. 1 Medium**	With a deep color and a stronger maple flavor, this is characterized by some as "caramel-like" and is usually made later in the season as the days get longer and warmer.	Some find it too assertive to be used as a table syrup, but its bolder flavor works well in baked goods.
Grade B	**No. 2 Amber; Commercial; No. 3 Dark**	A very dark, intensely flavored syrup; sometimes called "cooking syrup," this is made late in the season.	Some like its very strong maple flavor for a table syrup, but this is most often used for cooking and baking. Its boldness works well with meat glazes, candied yams, baked beans, and desserts that call for robust flavor.

Sap becomes syrup at 7° to 7.1°F above the boiling point of water. At sea level, water will boil at 212°F. For every 550-foot increase in elevation, the boiling point drops by 1°F. The correct temperature at which sap becomes syrup, therefore, varies with the location of the sugarhouse and to some degree with barometric pressure, which can also affect the exact boiling point. With late-winter weather conditions in maple country anything but stable — Mark Twain once commented that if you don't like our weather here in New England, just wait a minute — sugarmakers will regularly recheck the boiling point, even within the same day.

While an accurate temperature reading is an important guide to finished syrup, maple syrup produced for sale must be checked for proper density with a hydrometer. At room temperature, the standard density of syrup is 66 Brix, a scale sugarmakers use for measuring the percentage of sugar in syrup. A precise reading is important. Syrup with a density just a little below this range will taste thin and watery; a little above, and the syrup may become crystallized in storage. Because this finishing of syrup to just the right density is such an important step in the making of syrup, many sugarmakers transfer near-syrup to a special finishing pan, where this step can be carefully controlled, instead of completing the boiling process in the evaporator.

Once the syrup has been filtered to remove crystallized minerals, it is graded and hot-packed to prevent the growth of mold. Syrup is packaged by liquid measure into standard-sized containers, usually made of plastic or metal. The maple syrup, which by now has been reduced from as much as 40 parts of sap, is now ready for trading and sale.

Grading and Tasting

Though grading is not mandatory in all U.S. states, much of the maple syrup sold over the counter is assigned a grade. Grade is not an indicator of quality: It's determined to a large extent by color (as measured by light transmittance) but also by flavor. Some of the factors that account for grade are the sugar content of the sap, how quickly and at what point in the season it was collected and boiled, and the rate of evaporation.

A certain amount of confusion exists in regard to grading. This stems from the fact that grading terms have changed over the years. In addition, even though there are U.S. standards, some states have adopted their own grading language. For example, in Vermont, U.S. Grade A Light Amber is called "Vermont Fancy Grade." Canada and the United States have agreed on the same grading standards but use different terminology.

If I were to translate all of this grading into some practicable buying guidelines or suggestions for the cook, basically I'd say don't be too concerned about grades. Don't ignore the grade, because it will give you a clue as to the syrup's flavor and intensity. But the only way you'll ever find out just which grade you prefer for a particular use is to try a number of them. Let your taste buds be your guide. Just because a certain grade is supposedly best for cooking or baking doesn't mean you won't enjoy it on pancakes: Taste is a very individual matter.

For descriptions of the grades, refer to the chart (page 7). If you want to find out whether a particular U.S. state has its own grading system, contact that state's department of agriculture or maple producers association.

Some government entities and maple producers associations have established quality programs that entitle individual producers to use a special logo or symbol on their maple syrup. You may choose to look for such seals of approval, but to be sure you are buying 100 percent, pure maple syrup, you need only read the label carefully. Syrup blends, often labeled "pancake syrup," usually contain corn syrup with artificial maple extract, and those ingredients are listed on the label.

Substituting Maple Syrup

General cooking. Use only three-fourths the amount of maple syrup as sugar in a recipe. For example, if a recipe says to use ¼ cup (4 tablespoons) of sugar, use 3 tablespoons of maple syrup instead.

Baking. For every cup of sugar, substitute ¾ cup to 1½ cups maple syrup, and reduce the dominant liquid in the recipe by 2 to 4 tablespoons. Don't cut back on a liquid that is likely to alter the flavor or texture of a recipe, such as the liqueur, oil, or egg, when you have 2 cups of milk to play with.

You may also need to add ¼ to ½ teaspoon baking soda to reduce maple syrup's slight acidity; this will not be necessary in recipes with buttermilk, sour milk, or sour cream.

If you are serious about getting a recipe just right, measure your ingredients carefully and make notes where you've altered the recipe. Then, using your notes, try the recipe a second time if it doesn't work out as hoped, making the appropriate changes. Read the entire recipe through carefully before you begin, and see how it makes sense to proceed.

And as far as substituting maple syrup for honey, I've found you can almost always succeed with an equivalent substitution.

Maple in the Kitchen

I've never encountered storage problems with maple syrup, simply because it's used up very quickly around here. Generally speaking, however, syrup will keep best if it is transferred to clear, glass containers and kept cold. Freezing is the smartest option for long-term storage, one especially worth considering if your refrigerator space is limited. I know one woman who divides her occasional gallon purchase of syrup among four glass quart jars, leaving at least 1 inch of headspace for expansion of the syrup as it freezes, and freezing all but one jar. Then, when her refrigerator supply runs out, she takes another quart out of freezer storage.

While maple syrup stored in glass containers and refrigerated maintains its flavor indefinitely, care must be taken with syrup stored in tin. Tin cans rust, so be careful where in the refrigerator your container is placed. And, syrup in a tin package can pick up a tin flavor.

Syrup stored in plastic will usually maintain quality for three to six months. Because plastic breathes, a color and flavor change may result with long-term storage in plastic.

Over time, you may find mold growing on your syrup in the refrigerator. Don't throw it away. Rather, strain it through cheesecloth and then bring the syrup to a boil. Pour it back into a clean container, and your syrup will be perfectly safe to use. Also, if your syrup should crystallize, you can restore it to its liquid state by placing the container in a pan of very hot water; heating melts the crystals.

Cooking with Maple

Even with these recipes as your guide to maple syrup cooking and baking, sooner or later you may reach a point where you would like to strike out on your own. Perhaps you want to convert a family-favorite cookie recipe or adapt something you find in a new cookbook. How should you proceed?

Well, that all depends. Some recipes are easier to convert than others. A recipe that will end up in liquid form — say a sauce or beverage — is seldom a problem because the texture isn't likely to be too critical. Some cakes, on the other hand, have a precise balance of liquid to dry ingredients and can be difficult to get just right. Then, you also have to factor in that maple syrup not only adds a brownish tinge to whatever it is you're cooking but also tends to make baked goods brown more quickly than sugar does (reducing the oven temperature by 25°F sometimes compensates for that). Do you want that, and is it appropriate for what you're cooking?

Basically, you have to account for two things when substituting maple syrup for sugar in a recipe: that syrup is sweeter than sugar, and that it adds extra moisture to the recipe. General guidelines for substituting maple syrup are on page 9.

CHAPTER TWO

MAPLE MORNINGS

Start the day with the glory of pure maple syrup. From traditional pancakes, French toast, and waffles on top of which to pour lots of warm pure maple syrup to breakfast breads with maple goodness baked right in, what a way to greet the day. Try fruit favorites, sweet breads, and puddings that make tempting additions to any breakfast table. Make breakfast extra-special or wow brunch guests with tasty treats such as potato patties, spreads, and beverages.

HOT STUFF

Pancakes are precious little things, with little mass, so they begin to lose heat quickly once they're off the griddle. And cold pancakes, we all know, hold none of the promise and allure of a hot, steamy stack. Therefore, have warm plates waiting in the oven if at all possible (10 minutes in a 250°F oven will do the trick). Also, have your pancake eaters assembled nearby, and whisk them to the table as soon as the stacks hit the plates. Finally, have *soft* butter on the table. I always hate it when I forget this and have to watch somebody hack up a perfect stack, spreading a cold, hard pat of butter on a delicate pancake. It makes me cringe.

CLASSIC PANCAKES

These pancakes are like home to me. After I've been spinning off all sorts of pancake variations, they're comforting to come back to. They have an honest, grainy flavor; just the right amount of crunch; and a pleasant, cakey texture. Remember that whole-grain flours vary widely in their absorptive capabilities, so the batter may have to be thinned with a little milk to reach the proper consistency.

1 **cup cornmeal, preferably stone-ground**
1½ **cups whole-wheat flour**
½ **teaspoon salt**
1 **tablespoon baking powder**
3 **eggs**
1¾ **cups milk**
2 **tablespoons molasses**
¼ **cup oil or 4 tablespoons butter, melted**
Butter for greasing skillet
Warm pure maple syrup for drizzling on top

1. Stir together the cornmeal, flour, salt, and baking powder in a large bowl.

2. In a separate bowl, beat the eggs well and blend in the milk and molasses.

3. Make a well in the dry ingredients, then pour in the egg mixture and the oil. Stir just until smooth. Let the batter stand for several minutes before cooking.

4. Heat a large skillet or griddle over medium-high heat, then butter it lightly. Drop the batter by heaping tablespoonfuls and cook until the pancake bottoms are golden and bubbles are popping on the surface, about 1 minute. Turn and cook 1 minute on the other side. Keep warm (see Hot Stuff).

5. Repeat with remaining batter. Serve with warm maple syrup (page 17).

Yield: About 14 four-inch pancakes

Pancake Pointers

For all of their apparent simplicity, the ability to make good pancakes is an acquired skill. Murphy's Law applies, and things do go wrong. This point was brought home to me not long ago when I developed a number of pancake recipes for a food magazine — recipes I had tested to death in my home kitchen — only to hear back from their test kitchen that several of the recipes hadn't worked for them. In the end we worked out the bugs, and in the process I learned that foolproof pancake-making hinges on several important, basic principles. Let's look briefly at some of these variables.

The Batter

■ First and foremost, don't beat it. When you beat batter you develop the gluten, a wheat protein responsible for the formation of elastic strands. Beating toughens your pancakes and keeps them from achieving a light, fluffy texture. So just stir your liquids into the dry ingredients until they're blended. The best tool I've found for this is a simple wire whisk with widely spaced strands. A wooden spoon or spatula works fine, too.

■ Even though pancake recipes always give precise measurements for ingredients, it is quite common for the batter to need adjustment. Generally it needs to be thinned, and this is especially true with whole grains, since they absorb moisture gradually as the batter sits. After you've made a pancake recipe a number of times, you will learn the precise consistency and the pancake texture it will yield. Most pancake batters perform best when they are neither so thin that they run all over creation, nor so thick that you have to spread them around. I've found that my electric griddle produces better results with a slightly thicker batter, while my skillet works best with a thinner batter.

The Cooking Surface

■ Basically, the more metal you can put between your heat source and your pancakes, the better. A thick, heavy surface spreads the heat around, and the pancakes cook evenly, whereas a thin pan cooks spottily and you get "hot spots" on your pancakes. Cast iron is superb. I have a special cast-iron pancake skillet that I use only for making pancakes and warming tortillas. It has very low sides, so I can slide the spatula under the pancakes easily.

■ I really prefer to cook my pancakes on my old Farberware electric griddle, blackened from years of use. The advantage of electric is absolute and even heat control: I just set it at 375°F and go. Size is the other big plus. I can make six pancakes at a time on my electric griddle; about the most I can manage in even the largest skillet is three.

Cooking

■ It takes only an initial light rub of oil on your cooking surface to keep pancakes from sticking. After that, the fat in the batter prevents sticking.

■ Pancakes generally take about 1½ to 2 minutes to cook on side one, a little less on side two. When little air holes start to show up on the surface and the very edge takes on a dryish tinge, they're ready to flip. Only flip them once and avoid any inclination to poke, prod, or press on them — that spells disaster for pancakes.

TESTING THE PAN

When you're cooking pancakes with a burner and skillet, the standard readiness test is to sprinkle a drop of water in the pan. A very active response, sizzling and bouncing, is supposed to signal a sufficiently hot surface. A lukewarm, fizzling response means the pan is not hot enough. This water test is only so reliable, because there's no clear indication when the pan is too hot. You can use the water test to get an idea of where you stand, but expect to do the fine-tuning with your first pancake or two.

OATMEAL PANCAKES

My great friend Jeanne Lemlin, James Beard Award–winning author of several classics of inspired vegetarian cooking, gave me this recipe. Jeanne makes my kind of pancakes: grainy and nicely textured. You'll want to make these often once you've tried them.

       1 **cup old-fashioned rolled oats**
       1 **cup unbleached or all-purpose flour**
      ½ **cup whole-wheat flour**
     2½ **teaspoons baking powder**
       1 **teaspoon salt**
       2 **eggs**
       2 **cups milk**
       2 **tablespoons firmly packed brown sugar**
       5 **tablespoons butter, melted**
          Butter for greasing skillet
          Warm pure maple syrup for drizzling on top

1. Whirl the oats in a food processor or blender until they become a fine powder; a few traces of flakes are fine. Pour into a large bowl; then mix in the all-purpose and wheat flours, baking powder, and salt. Set aside.

2. In a medium-sized bowl, beat the eggs lightly, and then whisk in the milk and brown sugar.

3. Make a well in the dry ingredients, pour in the egg mixture, and stir briefly. Add the butter and blend just until no traces of dry are visible. Let the batter stand for several minutes.

4. Heat a large skillet or griddle over medium-high heat, then butter it lightly. Drop the batter by heaping tablespoonfuls and cook until the pancake bottoms are golden and bubbles are popping on the surface, about 1 minute. Turn and cook 1 minute on the other side. Keep warm (page 12).

5. Repeat with remaining batter. Serve with warm maple syrup (page 17).

Yield: About 14 four-inch pancakes

Banana-Nut Cakes

This recipe comes from Susan Cunningham, one of the owners of The Inn at Goodwin Park in Portsmouth, New Hampshire. Susan and company might serve these pancakes to their guests along with baked Frangelico-flavored pears.

1	cup unbleached or all-purpose flour
1	cup whole-wheat flour
2½	teaspoons baking powder
½	teaspoon baking soda
½	teaspoon salt
½	cup chopped walnuts or pecans
2	eggs
1⅓–1½	cups milk
¾	cup sour cream
¼	cup pure maple syrup
4	tablespoons butter, melted
1	ripe banana, mashed
	Butter for greasing skillet
	Warm pure maple syrup for drizzling on top

1. Combine the all-purpose and wheat flours, baking powder, baking soda, salt, and nuts in a large bowl. Toss to mix.

2. In a separate bowl, beat the eggs until frothy, then whisk in 1⅓ cups of the milk, the sour cream, maple syrup, butter, and banana. Add additional milk, a tablespoon at a time, to thin the batter, if needed. Make a well in the dry ingredients, then pour in the egg mixture. Stir, just to blend; do not beat. Let the batter stand for several minutes.

3. Heat a large skillet or griddle over medium-high heat, then butter it lightly. Drop the batter by heaping tablespoonfuls and cook until the pancake bottoms are golden and bubbles are popping on the surface, about 1 minute. Turn and cook 1 minute on the other side. Keep warm (page 12). Repeat with remaining batter. Serve with warm maple syrup (page 17).

Yield: About 14 four-inch pancakes

A WELL-SEASONED PAN

My special cast-iron pancake skillet has a glossy black seasoning built up from years of use. The seasoning acts as a sort of natural, nonstick finish, so I'm careful not to scrub it with anything abrasive. A gentle washing with a mild detergent is enough. After that I dry the skillet briefly over a hot flame, then I rub about ½ teaspoon of oil into the surface with a paper towel.

BUTTERMILK CORN CAKES

Here is a lovely buttermilk pancake, one I've been making for many years. It differs from other corn cakes in that the cornmeal is precooked, giving the pancakes a soft and moist, instead of cakey, texture.

1	cup cold water
½	cup cornmeal, preferably stone-ground
⅔	cup buttermilk
⅔	cup plus 1–2 tablespoons milk
¼	cup blackstrap molasses
2	eggs, lightly beaten
¼	cup butter, melted, or vegetable oil
1¼	cups whole-wheat flour
1½	teaspoons baking powder
½	teaspoon baking soda
½	teaspoon salt
	Butter for greasing skillet
	Warm pure maple syrup for drizzling on top

1. Stir together the water and cornmeal in a small, heavy-bottomed saucepan. Bring to a boil, reduce the heat to medium, and cook, stirring constantly, for 2 to 3 minutes, until quite thick. Scrape into a large bowl. Whisk in, one at a time, the buttermilk, milk, molasses, eggs, and butter.

2. Combine the flour, baking powder, baking soda, and salt in a separate large bowl. Toss to mix. Make a well in the dry ingredients, add the egg mixture, and stir just until blended. Let the batter stand for several minutes, then thin with a tablespoon or two of milk, if needed; the batter should run thickly off the ladle.

3. Heat a large skillet or griddle over medium-high heat, then butter it lightly. Drop the batter by heaping tablespoonfuls and cook until the bottoms are golden and bubbles are popping on the surface, about 1 minute. Turn and cook 1 minute on the other side. Keep warm (page 12). Repeat with remaining batter.

Yield: About 18 four-inch pancakes

Maple French Toast

In this variation on the classic French toast, maple syrup is added to the batter to infuse the bread with sweetness. A member of the Citadelle Maple Syrup Producers' Cooperative of Quebec, Canada, created this recipe.

> 2 eggs
> ⅔ cup milk
> ⅓ cup pure maple syrup
> 2 tablespoons cream
> ¼ teaspoon salt
> Dash of nutmeg
> 8 slices of bread, crusts trimmed
> Butter for greasing skillet
> Warm pure maple syrup, fruit preserves, or lemon juice and confectioners' sugar for topping

1. Beat the eggs until light. Whisk in the milk, maple syrup, cream, salt, and nutmeg to taste.

2. Dip slices of bread in the egg mixture, one at a time, turning to coat both sides.

3. Heat a large skillet or griddle over medium heat, then butter it lightly. Cook the bread for 2 to 3 minutes per side, or until golden brown. Keep warm (page 12).

4. Repeat with remaining bread and batter. Serve with warm maple syrup (see Syrup Warmer).

Yield: 3–4 servings

Syrup Warmer

If you want your syrup to go farther on pancakes and waffles, and don't want your food to get cold, warm the syrup up first, so it thins out. Warm syrup won't rob heat from your pancakes the way cold syrup will. You can heat your syrup in a saucepan over low heat (don't let it come to a boil) and spoon it out; keep a small amount in a table dispenser and warm that in a pan of hot water; or heat ½ cup of syrup in the microwave on HIGH for 30 to 60 seconds. I'm all in favor of those spring-loaded, glass dispensers you see in diners. Since the spring holds the top shut, there's no chance of accidentally spilling the valuable contents all over the table. This is especially useful if you have young kids. When our three were young, our breakfast table was a regular reach-a-rama. Stuff flew everywhere.

Citadelle Maple Syrup Producers' Cooperative

Though many people the world over still think "Vermont" when they hear the words *maple syrup,* Quebec is by far the largest producer in the world.

The Citadelle Maple Syrup Producers' Cooperative began in 1925, when 102 syrup producers united to cope with a monopoly of buyers whose low prices threatened to destroy the maple syrup market. Today, according to Richard Acheson of the cooperative, grandchildren of the founders are among the 2,700 producers in Quebec who are cooperative members.

The cooperative's members store the syrup they produce during the short maple season in specially designed vats, from which syrup is tested, refiltered, bottled, and shipped. In the U.S. market, Citadelle syrup is sold under the brand "Camp Maple Syrup."

Citadelle also works to promote 100 percent pure maple syrup by distributing recipes that show people how to use maple syrup for more than just pancakes. And, as part of its maple marketing program, in 1999 the cooperative opened a shop called Canadian Maple Delights. The combination gift shop–bistro features maple products for all occasions and light meals utilizing maple syrup as a prime ingredient.

"We're working on perfecting the existing shop and would like to open a few more in the years to come," Richard said. Until they do, you can visit them at their Web site. See page 132 for contact information. (Recipes from Citadelle members are on pages 17, 34, 56, 57, 91, and 128.)

WHOLE-WHEAT CORN WAFFLES

These wholesome waffles have a wonderful crunch and a deep, grainy flavor. They're great with a little plain yogurt on the side.

Butter for greasing waffle iron
1½ **cups whole-wheat flour**
½ **cup cornmeal, preferably stone-ground**
2 **tablespoons sugar**
4 **teaspoons baking powder**
¾ **teaspoon salt**
2 **eggs**
2⅓ **cups milk**
½ **cup (1 stick) butter, melted (or part butter and part vegetable oil)**
Warm pure maple syrup and plain yogurt, optional

1. Preheat a waffle iron and grease it lightly.

2. Combine the flour, cornmeal, sugar, baking powder, and salt in a large bowl. Toss to mix.

3. In a separate bowl, beat the eggs lightly. Whisk in the milk and butter. Make a well in the dry ingredients, then pour in the egg mixture. Whisk briefly, just until blended. Let the batter stand for several minutes.

4. Cook the batter in the prepared waffle iron until crisp and golden, about 2 minutes. Keep warm (page 12 and Waffle Thoughts).

5. Repeat with remaining batter. Serve with warm maple syrup (page 17) and yogurt, if desired.

Yield: 4–5 servings

WAFFLE THOUGHTS

There are certain things I like more about waffles than pancakes, the main thing being that they aren't so fussy. You can make up a batch of waffles and hold them in the oven on a wire rack for a reasonable amount of time — up to 15 minutes, say, at about 250°F — without having them turn to rubber like pancakes will. Waffles even taste great at room temperature, or slightly warm; pancakes don't. Therefore, leftover waffles are never a problem. You can even pop them in the toaster the next day to warm them up, and they'll regain at least some of their crispness. They're not quite the same as fresh, but you could do much worse.

FLOUR CHOICE

If you want to replace some or all of the whole-wheat flour in these recipes with all-purpose flour, reduce the main liquid in the recipe slightly, because whole-wheat flour is more absorptive than white flour.

DEATH BY CHOCOLATE WAFFLES

Well, maybe they're not *life* threatening, but they're surely diet threatening! Try these crisp, double-chocolate waffles with a small mountain of vanilla ice cream and a pool of maple syrup. The ultimate in chocolate decadence.

	Butter for greasing waffle iron
1⅓	cups unbleached or all-purpose flour
⅓	cup whole-wheat flour
¼	cup unsweetened cocoa
1	tablespoon baking powder
1	teaspoon cinnamon
½	teaspoon salt
½	cup (1 stick) butter
3	ounces semisweet chocolate
2	tablespoons sugar
2¼	cups milk
2	eggs, beaten until frothy
	Warm pure maple syrup

1. Preheat a waffle iron and grease it lightly. Combine the flours, cocoa, baking powder, cinnamon, and salt in a large bowl. Toss to mix. Set aside.

2. Combine the butter, chocolate, and sugar in a heavy-bottomed saucepan and melt over very low heat. Whisk to smooth, remove from the heat, then whisk in the milk and eggs.

3. Make a well in the dry ingredients, pour in the chocolate mixture, and blend, just until everything is combined; watch for dry clumps. Let the batter stand for several minutes; it will thicken slightly.

4. Cook the batter in the prepared waffle iron until crisp and golden, about 2 minutes. Keep warm (page 12 and 19). Repeat with remaining batter.

Yield: 4–5 servings

GRANOLA

Every Christmas I like to prepare large batches of this granola for my friends and family; it makes a great stocking stuffer. Instead of all oats you can also use other grain flakes. A portion of the seeds may be replaced with bran or untoasted wheat germ.

4   **cups old-fashioned oats**
1   **cup coarsely chopped nuts (cashews, pecans, or almonds)**
1   **cup raw (unroasted) sunflower seeds**
½   **cup sesame seeds**
½   **cup shredded unsweetened coconut (available in health food stores)**
½   **teaspoon salt**
6   **tablespoons pure maple syrup**
6   **tablespoons light-tasting vegetable oil, such as sunflower oil**
1   **cup chopped dried raisins or dates**

Granola Goodies

You can use your own preferences to adjust the mix of goodies in your granola. Just be sure that the substitutions and additions add up to approximately the same volume as in the recipe. Some delicious additions are dried mixed tropical fruits, dried cranberries or cherries, and slivered dried apricots; spices such as cinnamon, ginger, or cardamom; and wheat germ.

1. Preheat oven to 300°F. Toss the oats, nuts, sunflower seeds, sesame seeds, coconut, and salt to mix in a large bowl.

2. Combine the maple syrup and oil in a saucepan; warm over low heat. Pour over the oat mixture. Stir with a wooden spoon, then roll up your sleeves and work the mixture with your hands until everything is moistened.

3. Spread — no more than about ½ inch thick — on baking sheets and roast for 30 to 40 minutes, stirring occasionally, until golden.

4. Cool thoroughly, then stir in the raisins. Store in jars or plastic bags.

Yield: About 8 cups

Banana Crêpes in Maple Rum Sauce

Virgin syrup ... sugar worthy the table of the gods.

— John Burroughs,
In the Catskills

Whether for a special breakfast, brunch, or even dessert, this recipe is easy to make. If the bananas are large, three should be enough. The bananas could be served plain, but the crêpes make for an elegant presentation. For dessert, you can also serve the bananas on pound cake, topped with vanilla ice cream.

CRÊPES
- 1 cup unbleached all-purpose flour
- 1¾ cups milk
- 4 eggs
- 4 tablespoons butter, melted
- ½ teaspoon salt
- 2⅔ tablespoons butter for greasing skillet

BANANAS
- Butter for greasing skillet
- 4 small to medium bananas, peeled, halved lengthwise, and then crosswise
- 2 tablespoons butter
- ⅓ cup pure maple syrup
- ¼ cup dark rum
- 1 tablespoon lemon juice
- 4 slices pound cake
- Vanilla ice cream

1. **FOR THE CRÊPES:** In a food processor or blender, process the flour, milk, eggs, butter, and salt until smooth. Add more milk if necessary; the batter should have the consistency of light cream. Chill for at least 30 minutes.

2. Heat a small, nonstick skillet or crêpe pan over medium heat, then melt 1 teaspoon of butter in it. Spread the butter to cover the bottom and part of the sides of the pan.

3. Pour a little less than ¼ cup of the batter into the pan and quickly tip the pan, moving it in a circular fashion to evenly spread the batter over the bottom and sides. Cook for about 2 minutes; flip the crêpe and cook for 30 seconds longer.

4. Repeat with remaining batter. As you finish cooking the crêpes, stack them between sheets of wax paper to prevent them from sticking. (Crêpes may be frozen, unfilled; leave the wax paper between them.)

5. **FOR THE BANANAS:** Preheat oven to 375°F. Grease a large, ovenproof skillet or casserole dish and lay the bananas in it, flat side down. Set aside.

6. Melt the butter in a saucepan, then add the maple syrup. Bring to a boil, boil for a moment, then add the rum and lemon juice. As soon as the syrup returns to a boil, remove from the heat, and pour over the bananas. Place in the oven and bake for 15 minutes, basting once or twice.

7. Remove the bananas from the oven. Using a slotted spatula, transfer two banana slices to a crêpe and roll the crêpe; place on a dish. Repeat with remaining bananas to fill seven more crêpes (two per dish).

8. Put the skillet on the burner — or transfer the liquid to a saucepan if you used a casserole — and quickly reduce the liquid to a thick syrup, over high heat. Spoon the sauce over the crêpes.

Yield: 4 servings

WHERE TO TAP?

Among sugarmakers, there's no dearth of down-home wisdom regarding the placement of taps — "the higher (or lower) the tap, the sweeter the sap"; "tap the warm side of the tree"; "the older the tree, the sweeter the sap" — but studies have shown that tap location has little or no appreciable effect on yield. With each successive year, the position of new tapholes is staggered, to avoid hitting old tapholes or dead tissue, hidden by new bark, that may contribute to a reduced sap flow.

Maple-Walnut Oat Muffins

I love oats in breads. The subtle oat flavor really shines here, reinforced beautifully by a sweet maple note. Very fragrant, these muffins will draw a crowd to your kitchen at any hour.

1¼ **cups old-fashioned oats**
1 **cup whole-wheat flour**
½ **cup unbleached or all-purpose flour**
1 **teaspoon baking powder**
1 **teaspoon baking soda**
1 **teaspoon salt**
2 **eggs**
1 **cup buttermilk**
½ **cup pure maple syrup**
¼ **cup vegetable oil**
½ **cup finely chopped walnuts**

1. Preheat oven to 400°F. Grease a 12-cup muffin tin and set aside.

2. Process the oats in a food processor or blender until they are reduced to a coarse powder; it is fine if some larger flakes remain. Measure exactly 1 cup of this oat flour and combine it in a large bowl with the wheat and all-purpose flours, baking powder, baking soda, and salt. Toss to mix.

3. Beat the eggs in a separate bowl, then blend in the buttermilk, maple syrup, and oil. Make a well in the dry ingredients, pour in the egg mixture, and stir just to blend. Fold in the walnuts. Divide the batter evenly among the muffin cups.

4. Bake for 20 minutes, or until golden. Serve hot.

Yield: 12 muffins

Maple Bran Muffins

With these tasty morsels, Joan Lukes of Merrill, Wisconsin, took first place in the 1999 recipe contest sponsored by the Wisconsin Maple Syrup Producers Association.

- 1 cup flour
- 1 teaspoon baking soda
- 1 cup bran flakes
- ⅓ cup raisins
- ½ cup chopped walnuts, optional
- 1 cup pure maple syrup
- 1 cup sour cream
- 2 eggs

TOPPING
- 3 tablespoons all-purpose flour
- 2 tablespoons firmly packed brown sugar
- 1 tablespoon butter

1. Preheat oven to 400°F. Grease a 12-cup muffin tin and set aside.

2. Sift the flour and baking soda into a medium-sized bowl. Add the bran flakes, raisins, and walnuts, if desired.

3. Combine the maple syrup, sour cream, and eggs in a small bowl; add to the dry ingredients and stir until just blended. Fill the muffin cups three-quarters full with the mixture.

4. TO MAKE THE TOPPING: Combine the flour and sugar in a small bowl. Cut in the butter until the mixture is crumbly. Sprinkle the topping on the batter.

5. Bake for 15 to 20 minutes, or until the muffins are golden brown.

Yield: 12 muffins

MAPLE CREAM SCONES

These soft, delicate biscuits are one of the most delicious ways I know to run up your cholesterol count. You can imagine how good they are, since they call for both cream and butter. Served with coffee, they make a simple, satisfying breakfast.

> 2 **cups all-purpose or unbleached flour**
> 1 **tablespoon baking powder**
> ¾ **teaspoon salt**
> 4 **tablespoons cold butter, cut into ¼-inch pieces,**
>   **plus 2 tablespoons butter, melted**
> ¾ **cup heavy cream**
> ¼ **cup plus 2 tablespoons pure maple syrup**

1. Preheat oven to 425°F. Lightly grease a baking sheet.

2. Combine the flour, baking powder, and salt in a large bowl. Cut the butter pieces into the flour until the mixture resembles coarse crumbs. Make a well in the mixture.

3. Blend the cream and ¼ cup of the maple syrup and pour the mixture into the well. Stir, just until the dough coheres.

4. Lightly flour a work surface; turn the dough onto the surface and knead four or five times, gently. Pat or roll to a thickness of about ¾ inch. Cut into 2½-inch to 3-inch rounds with a biscuit cutter and place on the prepared baking sheet.

5. Stir together the melted butter and remaining 2 tablespoons maple syrup, then brush a little on each scone. Keep the remaining syrup mixture warm. Bake the scones for about 15 minutes, until golden. Serve hot. Spoon the remaining warm syrup mixture over the scones.

Yield: About 12 scones

Oven Apple Pancakes

I've always loved the rustic look of this pancake as much as I have the flavor. It's one of the prettier things you'll ever aim a jug of syrup at. Simple to make, too, for a fast breakfast or even a last-minute dessert. It puffs up beautifully in the oven but doesn't stay that way for long. You can serve this sliced, right from the skillet, or invert it onto a plate (first loosen underneath with a spatula).

- 2 firm cooking apples, peeled, cored, and sliced
- 2 tablespoons pure maple syrup
- 1 tablespoon lemon juice
- 4 tablespoons butter
- 3 eggs
- ½ cup milk or light cream
- ½ cup unbleached or all-purpose flour
- ½ teaspoon cinnamon
- ¼ teaspoon salt
  Warm pure maple syrup for drizzling on top

1. Preheat oven to 425°F. Toss the apples with the maple syrup and lemon juice and set aside. Melt the butter in a medium-sized cast-iron skillet and remove from the heat.

2. Beat the eggs and milk in a bowl with 1 tablespoon of the melted butter. In a separate bowl, combine the flour, cinnamon, and salt and whisk in the egg mixture until smooth.

3. Return the skillet to the heat and sauté the apples in the remaining butter over high heat. After 2 or 3 minutes, before they get mushy, spread the apples evenly in the pan and slowly pour on the batter. Bake for 15 to 18 minutes, until very puffy and lightly browned. Serve hot or warm directly from the pan, drizzled with maple syrup.

Yield: 4–6 servings

STICKY BUNS

If you like sticky buns but can seldom find the time to make the real thing, these are for you. I've taken an ordinary biscuit recipe and turned it into something quite extraordinary with the help of a maple glaze. And I seal the deal with a brown sugar, walnut, and cinnamon filling. You'll want to make these for a special Sunday breakfast.

½	**cup finely chopped walnuts**
¼	**cup firmly packed brown sugar**
½	**teaspoon cinnamon**
½	**cup pure maple syrup**
½	**cup (1 stick) plus 1 tablespoon cold butter**
2¼	**cups unbleached or all-purpose flour**
1	**tablespoon baking powder**
¾	**teaspoon salt**
1	**cup milk**

1. Preheat oven to 400°F. Mix together the walnuts, brown sugar, and cinnamon in a small bowl. Set aside.

2. In a small saucepan, bring the maple syrup and 4 tablespoons of the butter to a boil over medium heat. Boil for 30 seconds, then scrape into a 9-inch-square baking pan or a 10-inch deep-dish pie pan. Set aside.

3. Combine the flour, baking powder, and salt in a large bowl. Toss to mix. Cut 4 tablespoons of the butter into ½-inch pieces, add to the flour mixture, and cut it in until the butter is roughly the size of split peas. Make a well in the mixture and add the milk. Stir gently, just until the mixture forms a damp, cohesive mass. If the dough seems a bit wet, work in a tad more flour with the back of a wooden spoon. Melt the remaining 1 tablespoon butter in a small saucepan.

4. Turn the dough onto a lightly floured surface and knead gently, five or six times. Using a rolling pin, roll the dough into the best 9- by 12-inch rectangle you can manage; don't worry if it isn't perfect. Brush the surface with the melted butter.

5. Cover the dough evenly with the brown sugar mixture, patting it gently with your hands. Starting at the 9-inch edge, roll up the dough like a carpet, pinching at the seam to seal. Cut into nine 1-inch slices and lay them flat in the syruped pan. Bake for 25 minutes. Remove from the oven and invert onto a large plate; do this quickly, but carefully, being aware that the syrup is very hot. Oven mitts are a good precaution. Scrape any syrupy stuff from the pan and spread over the buns. Serve hot or warm.

Yield: 9 servings

Hot Cereals

As much as I love granola, nothing beats a bowl of hot cereal laced with real maple syrup or Fruit-Flavored Syrup (page 52) on a cold morning. Besides old-fashioned oats, try one of the following:

Grits. Any coarsely ground grain — such as soy, rye, or buckwheat — can be made into grits, not just the dried corn kernels of hominy grits.

Steel-cut oats. These oat groats are less processed than the old-fashioned or rolled oats commonly found in North American kitchens. They take longer to cook and have a chewy texture, but I love their heartiness. They are also called Scotch oats, Irish oatmeal, and porridge.

Triticale. A blend of wheat and rye, this grain has more protein and less gluten than wheat. It has a nutty-sweet flavor.

Applejack-Spiked Baked Apples

Most baked apples I can take or leave, but these — lavishly bathed in a heady combination of applejack, maple, butter, and vanilla — are in a class by themselves. One of the important steps here is to cool the apples, periodically basting them with the thickening juices, before you serve them. Excellent with a dollop of cold sour cream or lightly sweetened whipped cream.

¼ **cup finely chopped walnuts or pecans**
¼ **cup finely chopped dates**
3 **tablespoons butter**
4 **large baking apples**
⅓ **cup pure maple syrup**
¼ **cup water**
⅓ **cup applejack or ⅔ cup apple cider reduced over low heat to ⅓ cup**
1 **teaspoon vanilla extract**
¼ **teaspoon cinnamon**

1. Preheat oven to 375°F. Combine the walnuts and dates in a small bowl. Rub about ½ tablespoon of the butter into the nut mixture so it all pulls together. Set aside.

2. Core the apples, a little on the wide side, then peel the upper third of each one; this will help prevent them from bursting. Cut ¹⁄₁₆ inch off the bottom of each apple, so they sit flat in the pan. Divide the reserved nut mixture among the four cavities, stuffing it down into each one; hold one hand at the bottom so the mixture isn't pushed out. The filling should come to a little below the top of the apple, leaving a small space to hold the basting juice. Place the apples in a large pie dish.

3. Bring the maple syrup, water, and remaining 2½ tablespoons butter to a boil in a saucepan. Boil briefly, remove from the heat, then stir in the applejack, vanilla, and cinnamon. Pour this mixture over the apples, then put the pan in the oven. Bake for about 50 minutes, basting every 10 minutes or so. Remove from the oven and cool, periodically basting with the juices as they thicken. Serve lukewarm, at room temperature, or — my favorite way — cold, for breakfast. Spoon any leftover juice over the apples when served.

Yield: 4 servings

A Maple Lexicon

Ever wonder why maple syrup producers are called "sugarmakers" instead of "syrupmakers"? It's because the product made from maple sap was most often maple sugar, until white sugar became more widely available and less expensive. Here are some other terms associated with the magic of converting sap to maple products:

Buddy. Used to describe the unpleasant taste of sap that marks the end of the season.

Sugarbush. A grove of sugar maple trees; also called *sugar grove* or *sugar orchard*.

Sugar Camp. Before the advent of tubing that carried sap to a central sugarhouse, maple-sugaring sites were often set up in remote areas in the woods by Native Americans and early settlers.

Sugarhouse. A simple building, usually uninsulated, that shelters the boiling setup for a sugarbush. Sugarhouses have a vent in the roof, space for an evaporator, fuel, and sap storage. Today, many sugarhouses have restaurants or gift shops attached so visitors can watch the sugaring operation. Besides promoting tourism, these operations help keep alive the uniquely North American tradition of sugarmaking.

Sugar-off. The end of the season, when the sap has stopped running and the boiling is done.

PAN-FRIED APPLE RINGS

Here are three versions of apple rings: one plain, one saucy, and one crunchy. All are wonderful. They're sweet enough that, for breakfast, you wouldn't want to serve them with anything else sweet. They're best with breakfast meats, eggs, or yogurt. The crunchy version, with a graham cracker topping, could almost be considered a dessert, or a one-dish breakfast. Think of apple crisp, with lots of graham crackers in the topping — that's what it's like.

> 1 large, firm cooking apple, cored
> ½ cup water
> ⅓ cup pure maple syrup
> 2 tablespoons butter

1. Trim a little off the ends of the apple, then cut the apple into slices a scant ½ inch thick; you'll have five or six slices. Set aside.

2. Heat the water, maple syrup, and butter in a heavy, medium-sized skillet. Stir to blend, bringing the mixture to a boil. When it reaches a boil, add the apple rings, in one layer.

3. Reduce the heat to a low to moderate boil and cook, uncovered, until the liquid is reduced to a thick syrup, turning the rings several times to glaze them. Watch that the apples don't get mushy and that the syrup doesn't burn. Transfer to a serving plate, scraping the remaining glaze over them. Serve hot or warm.

APPLE RINGS WITH MAPLE CREAM SAUCE

1. Prepare and cook the apples as above. Before the syrup starts to coat the pan very thickly, transfer the rings to a warm plate, then pour ½ cup of light cream into the pan. Bring to a boil and cook, stirring constantly, for 15 seconds.

2. Reduce the heat to an active simmer and cook, stirring, for a minute or two longer. The finished sauce will have the consistency of heavy cream. Be careful to avoid burning the sauce. Spoon the hot sauce over the rings and serve immediately.

APPLE RINGS WITH GRAHAM CRACKER–CRUMB TOPPING

1. Before you begin, gently heat 2 tablespoons butter with 1 tablespoon maple syrup in a small saucepan, just until the butter melts. Stir in ¾ cup fine graham cracker crumbs; continue stirring until the mixture is smooth. Remove from the heat and set aside.

2. Preheat the broiler. Cook the apple rings as above. When heavily glazed, remove from the heat and spread the reserved crumbs evenly over the apples. Broil briefly, just until crumbs darken a shade or two. Watch carefully so the topping doesn't burn. Serve hot or warm.

Yield: 2–3 servings

Maple Nutrition

In addition to tasting great, pure maple syrup offers some nutritional benefits.

Sugar, an important source of energy, is the main nutrient. The main sugar in pure maple syrup and the sole sugar in the highest-grade syrup is sucrose. Darker grades have varying amounts of sucrose, fructose, and glucose. Glucose is the sweetest sugar, with fructose next, and sucrose less sweet.

Calories. Maple syrup has about 50 calories per tablespoon.

Minerals. Pure maple syrup has calcium (13.4 mg per tablespoon), potassium (40.8 mg per tablespoon), magnesium, manganese, phosphorus, and iron.

Vitamins. Trace amounts of B_2 (riboflavin), B_5 (pantothenic acid), niacin, and folic acid. And no cholesterol.

Spiced Maple Pears

A delicious alternative to baked apples, these pears are as good for dessert as they are for breakfast. A member of Quebec's Citadelle Maple Syrup Producers' Cooperative contributed this recipe.

- 2 cinnamon sticks
- 6 ripe pears, peeled with stems in place
- 6 cloves
- 8 cracked cardamom seeds
- 2 cups medium-sweet white wine
- ¾ cup pure maple syrup
- 2 tablespoons sugar

1. Preheat oven to 400°F. Place the cinnamon sticks in a deep 2-quart casserole dish. Push a clove inside each pear and lay them on their sides in the dish. Scatter the cardamom seeds on top of the pears.

2. In a medium saucepan over low heat, gently cook the wine, maple syrup, and sugar until the sugar is dissolved. Pour the mixture over the pears, ensuring that they are half covered (add more wine or water, if necessary).

3. Cover the pears and poach for 45 minutes to 1 hour, or until tender, basting occasionally. Remove the cloves, cardamom seeds, and cinnamon sticks. Cool slightly before serving; they may also be served chilled or at room temperature.

Yield: 6 servings

LEMON-MAPLE ZUCCHINI BREAD

I've come to think of zucchini bread recipes as the equivalent of public service messages you hear on the radio: They're helpful, even though we have become indifferent to them by overexposure. But I do think this moist, maple variation is particularly good and definitely worth a try next time the annual summer zucchini invasion rolls around.

3	**eggs**
1	**cup pure maple syrup**
½	**cup vegetable oil**
1	**teaspoon vanilla extract**
	Zest of 1 lemon, finely grated
1½	**cups grated zucchini or yellow summer squash**
1½	**cups unbleached or all-purpose flour**
1	**cup whole-wheat flour**
1	**tablespoon baking powder**
½	**teaspoon salt**

1. Preheat oven to 350°F. Grease a 9- by 5-inch loaf pan and set aside.

2. Beat the eggs with an electric mixer for 2 minutes. Gradually add the maple syrup, oil, vanilla, and lemon zest. Stir in the zucchini.

3. Combine the unbleached and wheat flours, baking powder, and salt in a large bowl. Make a well in the center, then stir in the zucchini mixture. Blend just until smooth, then turn into the prepared pan. Bake for 50 to 60 minutes, until a tester inserted into the center comes out clean. Cool in the pan for 5 to 10 minutes, then remove and cool completely on a wire rack.

Yield: 1 large loaf

MAPLE THOUGHTS

In his essay "Phases of Farm Life," American naturalist John Burroughs says of sugar-making, "Before the bud swells, before the grass springs, before the plow is started, comes the sugar harvest. It is the sequel of the bitter frost; a sap-run is the sweet good-by of winter."

— John Burroughs,
"Phases of Farm Life"

GOLDEN CORNMEAL CAKE

Here's a special-occasion breakfast cake worth rolling out of bed for. Sometimes I decrease the amount of coconut and add chopped walnuts.

- 1 cup (2 sticks) butter, softened
- 1 cup pure maple syrup, at room temperature
- 3 eggs, at room temperature
- 2 teaspoons vanilla extract
  Zest of 1 orange, finely grated
- 1¼ cups unbleached or all-purpose flour
- ¾ cup cornmeal, preferably stone-ground
- 1 tablespoon baking powder
- ½ teaspoon salt
- 1½ cups shredded, sweetened coconut
- ¾ cup sour cream
- 1 cup raisins

1. Preheat oven to 350°F. Grease a large tube pan or a 10-inch bundt pan and set aside.

2. Cream the butter with an electric mixer, gradually adding the maple syrup. Beat in the eggs, one at a time, then the vanilla and orange zest.

3. In a separate bowl, sift the flour, cornmeal, baking powder, and salt. Toss in the coconut. Add the dry ingredients to the butter mixture alternately with the sour cream, in two or three stages, each time just stirring to blend. Don't beat it. Fold in the raisins. Bake for 50 to 60 minutes, until a tester inserted into the center comes out clean. Cool briefly in the pan, then turn onto a plate and serve.

Yield: 12 or more servings

Pineapple Spice Upside-Down Cake

This is incredibly good: pineapples slices paired with Buttermilk Maple Spice Cake. I love the mapley-good stuff that runs between the pineapple slices, especially near the edge, where it turns to goo/crunch. Instead of pineapple, you might want to try fresh apple rings, or peeled peach or pear halves, flat side down in the pan.

- 1 recipe Buttermilk Maple Spice Cake (page 120),
  liquid and dry ingredients separated
- 7 canned pineapple slices (rings)
- 4 tablespoons butter
- ⅓ cup pure maple syrup
- ⅓ cup sugar
  Whipped cream, optional

1. Preheat oven to 350°F. Prepare the cake recipe, but do not mix the wet and dry ingredients together yet.

2. Blot the pineapple slices dry and set them aside.

3. Melt the butter in a medium-sized cast-iron skillet. Stir in the maple syrup and bring to a boil. Boil for 1 minute, stir in the sugar, and boil for 1 minute longer. Remove from the heat and arrange the pineapple slices in the pan — one in the center and the remaining slices around it. Set aside.

4. Make a well in the dry ingredients and add the liquids. Stir, just until blended. Pour the cake batter over the pineapple slices.

5. Bake for 30 minutes, until a tester inserted into the center comes out clean. Remove from oven and let sit for 2 minutes. Put a plate on top of the cake and invert. Serve hot or warm, with whipped cream, if desired.

Yield: 8 servings

MAPLE CRANBERRY-NUT COFFEE CAKE

The Wisconsin Maple Syrup Producers Association, like many similar sugarmakers' organizations, offers recipes using maple syrup to show people that maple syrup is not just for pancakes. No wonder they chose this one — it's a keeper.

2¼	teaspoons active dry yeast
1	cup warm (105°F–115°F) water
¼	cup pure maple syrup
2	tablespoons oil
1	tablespoon buttermilk powder
1	teaspoon grated orange zest
1	teaspoon salt
3–3½	cups all-purpose flour
⅓	cup dried cranberries
⅓	cup walnuts, chopped and toasted

MAPLE GLAZE

¼	cup pure maple syrup
2	tablespoons confectioners' sugar
1	tablespoon butter

1. Lightly oil a large bowl; set aside. In another large bowl, dissolve the yeast in the warm water. Add the maple syrup, oil, buttermilk powder, orange zest, and salt. Mix well.

2. Stir 1 cup of the flour into the mixture. Gradually stir in, ½ cup at a time, as much of the remaining flour as needed to make a soft dough. Blend in the cranberries and nuts. Knead for 5 to 10 minutes, or until smooth.

3. Put the dough into the greased bowl, turning once to coat. Cover, set in a warm draft-free place, and let rise until doubled in bulk, about 1 hour.

4. Punch down the dough and turn it onto a lightly floured surface.

5. Shape it into a 14- by 6-inch oval using your hands or a rolling pin. Using a pizza cutter or sharp knife, make two slices to cut the dough lengthwise into three strips. Braid the strips; with water or milk, lightly moisten the ends to firmly attach them to each other.

6. Carefully place the braid on a nonstick or lightly oiled baking sheet. Cover with a clean, lightweight cloth; let rise until doubled in bulk, about 45 minutes.

7. Preheat oven to 350°F. Uncover the braid and bake for 25 to 30 minutes, or until lightly browned. Cool slightly.

8. **TO MAKE THE GLAZE:** Combine the maple syrup, confectioners' sugar, and butter in a small saucepan. Bring to a boil, stirring, to form a smooth, spreadable glaze. Frost the warm loaf with the glaze or with Maple Butter Frosting (page 123).

Note: This recipe can be prepared in a bread machine. Make sure all ingredients are at room temperature; add ingredients in the order specified in the owner's manual for your bread machine. Add fruit and nuts at the appropriate time for your machine. Set the bread machine on the dough cycle. Allow the machine to run its cycle, adding flour and water to adjust dough as needed. Continue with steps 5 through 8 to complete the bread.

Yield: Makes 1 loaf

Sugaring-off Party

Friends and neighbors often gathered, out in the woods at the sugar camp or sugarhouse in many cases, to celebrate the end of the maple-sugaring season, a tradition still observed by many sugarmakers.

Lots of maple syrup is served, along with fresh-made maple cream and taffy. Other foods customarily served at the gatherings include maple-glazed ham, pickles — to counter the sweetness — and doughnuts, for dipping in fresh syrup.

Maple Bread Pudding

When the Massachusetts Maple Producers Association got together to publish recipes featuring pure maple syrup from the Bay State, Bill Schneider of Browning Brook Maple submitted this stovetop version of bread pudding. It's a great breakfast dish, or even dessert, especially when your oven is in use for another item on your menu.

- ¾ **cup pure maple syrup**
- 1 **tablespoon butter, softened**
- 4 **thick slices of bread, without crusts**
- ½ **cup chopped walnuts, pecans, or raisins**
- 1 **teaspoon lemon juice**
- 2 **cups milk**
- 2 **eggs**
- ¼ **teaspoon salt**
- ¼ **teaspoon vanilla extract**

1. Pour the maple syrup in the top of a double boiler. Butter each slice of bread, then cube. Add bread to the syrup, along with the nuts and lemon juice.

2. In a medium-sized bowl, beat the milk, eggs, salt, and vanilla and pour over the bread mixture. Do not stir, but press the bread down with a fork so that it is thoroughly moistened.

3. Set over gently boiling water and cook, uncovered, for 1 to 1¼ hours, or until a knife inserted into the top of the pudding comes out clean. Add more boiling water to the bottom pan as needed.

4. The pudding makes its own sauce; spoon it over each serving.

Yield: 4–6 servings

LACY SWEET-POTATO PATTIES

These savory pancakes are designed to be served with just a drizzle of maple syrup, so they're a good choice when you're not in the mood for an overly sweet breakfast. They go well with almost any egg dish, a side of applesauce, breakfast meats, toast, and biscuits. The pancake mixture isn't terribly cohesive, but as long as you don't manhandle the patties, or make them overly huge, they'll hold together just fine.

1 large sweet potato (about ½ pound)
¼ teaspoon salt
1 egg
2 tablespoons heavy or light cream
1 tablespoon cornmeal
½ cup minced ham or Canadian bacon
1 tablespoon minced onion
Freshly ground black pepper
Salt
Oil and butter for frying

1. Wash the sweet potato and remove any bad spots, then grate it into a bowl. Mix in the salt and set aside for 5 minutes.

2. While that sits, beat the egg lightly in a large bowl, then whisk in the cream and cornmeal. Using your hands, squeeze the moisture out of the grated potato, then add the potato to the egg mixture. Stir in the ham, onion, and pepper and salt to taste.

3. Heat about 1 tablespoon of oil in a heavy skillet over medium heat. Add 1 tablespoon of butter, let it melt, then — using about ¼ cup of the patty mixture per pancake — spoon the mixture into the skillet; don't crowd the pancakes. Spread and flatten the patties with a fork to a thickness of about ¼ inch. They should be no wider than your spatula. Fry for 3 to 4 minutes per side, flipping only once; they'll be dark and crusty on the outside. Serve hot. The patties hold up for a little while in a hot oven, if you want to serve them all at once.

Yield: 3–4 servings

Fried Mush/Polenta

I love corny things, and these luscious slices — dredged in cinnamon-spiked cornmeal, delicately fried in butter, then doused with maple syrup — are high on my list of breakfast favorites. They're perfect with breakfast meats and eggs, or with applesauce, berries, or yogurt on the side. A few other things to know: You must start this the night before. This will keep in the refrigerator for several days, so you can slice and fry anytime. And be sure to use fresh, stone-ground cornmeal, available in health food stores.

4	**cups water**
1	**teaspoon salt**
2	**cups cornmeal, preferably stone-ground**
	About 3 tablespoons butter
1½	**teaspoons cinnamon**
	Pure maple syrup for drizzling on top

1. Grease a large, shallow casserole, measuring either 8 by 12 inches or 9 by 13 inches.

2. Heat the water in a large, heavy-bottomed pot. Add the salt. As the water heats, sprinkle in 1½ cups of the cornmeal, a little at a time, whisking all the while. When the mixture reaches a boil, switch to a wooden spoon. Reduce the heat to medium-low and cook the mush, stirring continuously, for 15 minutes; the mixture will become quite thick. Stir in 1 tablespoon of the butter until melted, then remove from the heat.

3. Immediately scrape the mush into the prepared casserole and flatten the top as best you can with a spatula. Cool to room temperature, cover, and refrigerate overnight.

4. The next morning, stir the cinnamon into the remaining ½ cup cornmeal. Cut the chilled cornmeal mush into serving-size pieces — roughly 2 by 3 inches is a good size, but anywhere thereabouts is fine. Melt the remaining 2 tablespoons butter in a cast-iron skillet over medium-low heat. Dredge the slices in the cinnamon mix, then fry them in the butter, without crowding, 3 to 4 minutes on each side. Serve hot, drizzled with maple syrup.

Yield: 8 servings

Syrup by the Numbers

Some people find the price difference between pure maple syrup and maple-flavored pancake syrup (generally about 98% to 100% corn syrup) startling. Thinking about what it takes to produce the real thing puts that into perspective.

It takes four maple trees, at least 40 years old, to yield enough sap in 6 weeks to produce 1 gallon of maple syrup. Think about collecting and transporting that sap to the sugarhouse for boiling.

It takes about 40 gallons of sap, boiled down in an evaporator, to produce 1 gallon of syrup. On a smaller scale, that means it takes 2 gallons of sap to produce 1 cup of syrup. Comparing that to milk: that's two big jugs of milk to make one school-lunch milk carton.

It takes about one cord of wood or 60 gallons of oil to boil 800 gallons of syrup. Depending on the size of the evaporator used, that would require anywhere from 2 hours to 2 days.

BIRCH BUCKETS

Sap buckets in one form or another have been used in the collection of maple sap for some three hundred years. One early observer of the Native Americans describes their sap buckets, which were "fashioned from birch bark, cut and folded at the corners . . . and seamed with pine resin. The buckets were of various sizes, though usually held from 1 to 2 gallons."

CANADIAN BACON CHEESE DREAM

Reading through some old James Beard columns, I came across a reference to a once-popular sandwich he called a Cheese Dream — a combination of Cheddar cheese, sliced tomato, and bacon. Inspired by that thought, I spun off this breakfast version, and let me tell you, our friends with the golden arches have nothing on this. If your tomatoes aren't garden fresh, they might benefit from a quick flash in the pan with the bacon.

1½ **tablespoons pure maple syrup**
1 **tablespoon water**
2 **teaspoons lemon juice or cider vinegar**
1½ **teaspoons Dijon mustard**
Pinch of ground cloves
Pinch of cayenne
1 **tablespoon butter**
2 **thick slices Canadian bacon**
1 **English muffin, halved and toasted**
2 **eggs fried, over hard**
2 **thick slices tomato**
1 **cup grated Cheddar cheese, preferably smoked**

1. In a small bowl, whisk together the maple syrup, water, lemon juice, mustard, cloves, and cayenne. Set aside.

2. Melt the butter in a heavy skillet over medium heat and add the bacon. Fry gently, about 1 minute per side, then pour in the sauce. Increase the heat and continue to cook until the liquid reduces to a thick glaze. Remove from the heat.

3. Preheat the broiler. Place the toasted muffin halves in a pie plate. Swish the bacon slices in the glaze, then lay a slice on each muffin half. Top each with a fried egg and a slice of tomato, then spread the cheese over the top. Broil just until the cheese melts. Serve at once.

Yield: 2 servings

MAPLE-BACON STRATA

When Dianne Cutillo, my editor at Storey Books, invites friends over for brunch, this is one of her guests' favorites. You'll need to begin preparing it a day ahead.

½   pound bacon, chopped into ¼-inch pieces
1¼ cups heavy cream
1   cup milk
½   cup pure maple syrup
5   eggs
1   teaspoon Dijon mustard
1   teaspoon crumbled dried sage
1   teaspoon salt
8   slices (each 1-inch thick) sweet Portuguese bread
    or challah, lightly toasted and cut into thirds
12 ounces sharp Cheddar cheese, grated
⅔   cup chopped pistachio nuts

1. Grease a 2-quart casserole and set aside.

2. Cook the bacon pieces in a medium-sized skillet over medium-high heat until they are crisp, about 10 minutes. Drain on paper towels. Set aside.

3. Whisk together the cream, milk, maple syrup, eggs, mustard, sage, and salt.

4. Lay half of the bread in the prepared dish. Sprinkle it with half of the bacon, half of the cheese, and half of the nuts. Continue layering with remaining ingredients.

5. Pour the egg mixture over the layers, cover, and refrigerate overnight.

6. Remove the casserole from the refrigerator 30 minutes before baking. Preheat oven to 350°F. Uncover the dish and bake about 40 minutes, or until bubbly and golden.

7. Remove from the oven and let stand for 10 minutes before serving.

Yield: 8 servings

MEASURING TIP

Syrup often sticks to the sides of measuring cups and spoons. To make it easier to measure and pour (and to waste less), grease the cup or spoon lightly or coat with vegetable cooking spray before measuring.

WINTER SQUASH SPOONBREAD

Spoonbread is somewhere between a soufflé and cornbread, based on a thick sauce known as a *rick*. Here, I put puréed winter squash — acorn, butternut, or even pumpkin — into the rick with a little maple syrup. This puffs up nicely, but it doesn't stay that way long once it comes out of the oven. It is very good cold, for breakfast, with a little cream and maple syrup drizzled over it. But it's also a fine accompaniment to poultry dishes.

1½   cups peeled and diced winter squash,
      (½-inch pieces)
⅓   cup pure maple syrup
2   cups milk
1   cup cornmeal, preferably stone-ground
¾   teaspoon salt
⅛   teaspoon nutmeg
4   tablespoons butter, cut into ½-inch pieces
5   eggs, separated

1. Preheat oven to 375°F. Grease a large, shallow casserole and set aside.

2. Put the squash into a large saucepan with plenty of water. Bring to a boil, cover, then simmer for about 20 minutes, until the squash is very soft. Drain in a colander for several minutes, then purée the squash with the maple syrup in a food processor or blender. Set aside.

3. Pour the milk in a large, heavy-bottomed pot. Gradually whisk in the cornmeal over low heat. Turn the heat to medium-high and cook the cornmeal, stirring, until it starts to thicken, about 3 to 5 minutes. Reduce the heat slightly and continue to stir and cook for several more minutes, until it is quite thick.

4. Stir in the salt, nutmeg, butter, and squash mixture; whisk until smooth. Remove from the heat and whisk in the egg yolks. Pour into a large bowl.

5. Beat the egg whites until stiff, then fold them into the cooked mixture. Pour into the prepared pan and bake for about 35 minutes, until golden and puffed; large cracks will appear on the surface. Serve hot or very warm.

Yield: 8 servings

MAPLE BUTTER

Traditional maple butter, more commonly called maple cream, requires heating syrup to just the right temperature, cooling it to just the right temperature, then beating it to a creamy, thick consistency. This simpler version still makes a delicious spread for toast, muffins, and sweet breads.

> ½ **cup (1 stick) butter, softened**
> **Pinch of salt**
> ¼ **cup pure maple syrup**

1. In a food processor or with an electric mixer, whip the butter and salt until light and fluffy.

2. With the motor running, slowly pour the maple syrup through the feed tube of the food processor until the syrup is well incorporated. (If using an electric mixer, dribble the syrup into the butter while beating constantly.) Adding the syrup slowly and beating constantly will prevent the mixture from separating. The spread may be refrigerated, in a covered container, for up to 3 weeks.

Yield: About ¾ cup

PINEAPPLE-PEACH BUTTER

Pineapples and peaches, I think, are two fruits that combine especially well with maple, and that's why I like this butter. Use it to top vanilla ice cream or pancakes. Or stir it into plain yogurt for a quick, intense fruit lift.

- **3** pounds ripe peaches
- **2** cans (20 ounces each) unsweetened crushed pineapple
- **½** cup water
- **¼** cup lemon juice
- **1** cinnamon stick
- **½** cup pure maple syrup

1. Bring a medium-sized pot of water to a boil. Drop in the peaches, several at a time, and let the water come back to a boil. Boil for 15 seconds, then remove the peaches with a slotted spoon.

2. When cool enough to handle, slip off the skins and cut the peach flesh into chunks. Transfer to a large, nonreactive pot and add the pineapple and its juice, water, lemon juice, and cinnamon stick. Bring to a boil over moderate heat. Reduce the heat, cover partially, and simmer gently for 30 minutes, stirring occasionally, until the peaches are very soft. Remove from the heat and take out the cinnamon stick.

3. Preheat oven to 350°F.

4. Purée the fruit in a food processor or blender. Add the maple syrup and pulse to combine. Scrape the mixture into a large, nonreactive casserole dish.

5. Cook in the oven for as long as 2 hours, stirring occasionally, until the mixture is reduced by about half.

6. Refrigerate, tightly covered, for up to 4 weeks. If desired, pack the butter into four half-pint, sterilized canning jars and process for 10 minutes in a boiling-water bath according to the instructions provided by the manufacturer of the jar.

Yield: 2 pints

MAPLE–CREAM CHEESE SPREAD

Reducing maple syrup by cooking it before combining it with cream cheese prevents the mixture from separating. The Maine Maple Producers Association, which created this recipe, says that this spread can be stored, refrigerated and tightly covered, "for a long time — if it lasts." It doesn't last long in my house.

> ½ **cup pure maple syrup**
> 6 **ounces cream cheese, softened**

1. Simmer the maple syrup in a small saucepan over medium-low heat, stirring occasionally, until it is thickened to the texture of heavy honey — about 235°F on a candy thermometer. Do not overcook, or the syrup will not mix smoothly into the cream cheese.

2. Let the maple syrup cool slightly, stirring once or twice, then beat it into the cream cheese. Store tightly covered in the refrigerator.

Yield: About 1 cup

Using Flavored Butter and Cream Cheese

Maple butter and maple–cream cheese lift everyday foods out of the ordinary, so don't limit their use to breads, bagels, and crackers. Here are some ideas to inspire:

■ Stir dried cranberries or raisins or chopped dried apricots, apples, pineapples, or dates into maple butter or maple–cream cheese and spread on celery or crackers.

■ Spread maple butter or maple–cream cheese on apple or pear slices for a healthier alternative to cheese and crackers. Dip the fruit into a bowl of water containing 2 tablespoons of lemon juice to prevent browning.

■ Create sandwich sensations: Use maple–cream cheese instead of mayonnaise on a turkey sandwich. How about a maple butter and jelly sandwich?

■ Instead of a rich sauce, top broiled fish, chicken, or pork with a dab of maple butter.

MAPLE SAP COFFEE

Many a sugarmaker prepares coffee with raw maple sap, which Native Americans called "maple water," because it imparts a slightly sweet maple taste to the coffee. For the same reason, maple sap can also be used to make wine and beer.

MAPLE HOT CHOCOLATE

Properly speaking, *hot chocolate* is made with melted chocolate and *hot cocoa* with cocoa powder, though many folks use the terms interchangeably. Whatever way you like it, maple makes it more special.

　1　**cup whole milk**
　2　**ounces (2 squares) semisweet or bittersweet chocolate**
　1　**teaspoon pure maple syrup**
　　　Whipped cream or marshmallow cream, optional

1. Heat the milk and chocolate in a double boiler over simmering water until the chocolate is melted and well incorporated; do not boil.

2. Remove from heat; stir in the maple syrup. Pour into a mug and top with whipped cream, if desired.

Yield: 1 large or 2 small servings

LEMON-LIME HERBAL COOLER

I drink gallons of this sort of thing in the summertime. There's a lot of flexibility here, as far as what kind of herbal tea you can use. Lemon is probably my favorite, but I've also used orange- and raspberry-flavored herbal teas, and chamomile and peppermint, too. Don't let the tea steep for more than 5 minutes, or you'll overpower the maple flavor.

　8　**bags lemon or other herbal tea**
　2　**quarts boiling water**
　¼　**cup fresh lime juice (from about 2 medium limes)**
　¾–1　**cup pure maple syrup**
　　　Sprigs of fresh mint, if available
　　　Ice cubes (approximately 2 cups)

1. Put the tea bags in a large (not plastic) bowl and pour in the water. Steep for 5 minutes and then remove the tea bags with a slotted spoon.

2. Stir in the lime juice, maple syrup, and mint, and cool to room temperature. Remove the mint and transfer the liquid to a large jug. Add the ice cubes, cover, and refrigerate if not using right away.

Yield: About ½ gallon

MAPLE YOGURT SMOOTHIE

There are, of course, almost unlimited possibilities for maple smoothies. I've used bananas here, but soft berries in season are also terrific; any soft fruit will work. You can make spiked versions, by adding a compatible spirit or liqueur — Kahlua would be good here, for instance. Let your imagination guide you, bearing in mind the proportions of yogurt to maple and fruit.

> 1 **cup plain yogurt**
> ½ **cup milk**
> ⅓ **cup pure maple syrup**
> 1 **ripe banana, peeled**
> **Pinch of cinnamon**
> **Several ice cubes, crushed**

1. Combine the yogurt, milk, maple syrup, banana, and cinnamon in a blender.

2. Add the crushed ice and process until smooth. It's fine if shards of ice remain after the blending. Serve at once.

Note: To crush the ice cubes, put them in the folds of a tea towel and shatter with a hammer.

Yield: 2 servings

Fruit-Flavored Syrup

There's nothing wrong with drizzling pure maple syrup over ice cream, pound cake, pancakes, or waffles, but infusing the syrup with fruit flavor brings out the best of both. This is one area where it's easy to be creative. Mix and match the fruit and optional ingredients to create a signature syrup.

> 2　cups chopped, ripe fruit (pears, pineapple, peaches, plums, or apricots) or 2 cups berries (raspberries, blueberries, or strawberries)
> 1　cup pure maple syrup
> 1　teaspoon finely grated peeled fresh ginger root or 1 vanilla bean, split in half lengthwise, optional

1. In a food processor or blender, process the fruit, maple syrup, and ginger, if desired, until the mixture is puréed.

2. Pour the mixture into a small saucepan. If using a vanilla bean, scrape the seeds into the mixture. Simmer over low heat for 5 minutes.

3. Using a fine-meshed sieve or a double layer of cheesecloth in a strainer, strain the syrup, pressing fruit with the back of a spoon to extract as much liquid as possible. Serve immediately or refrigerate and reheat before serving.

Yield: About 1½ cups

CHAPTER THREE

BEYOND BREAKFAST

If you need proof that maple adds magic to just about any food, look no further. Whether in a spicy soup, tangy salad, or barbecue sauce, the flavor of maple will enliven your taste buds. And sugar maple combined with the gifts of the garden make for exceptional side dishes.

In main dishes, maple is less likely to be used as a sweetener than as a distinctive ingredient on its own. You'll love how it pairs with ingredients such as vinegar, citrus juice, pepper, and strong spices, filling your lunch, dinner, and snack plates with flavor.

SWEET POTATO AND BACON BISQUE

What a wonderful, cold-weather soup this is! The maple lifts the sweetness and flavor of the sweet potatoes, while the bacon and onion add depth and contrast. Excellent with cornbread or corn muffins and a mixed green salad served with a mustard vinaigrette.

4	cups peeled, diced sweet potatoes
4	cups water
6	bacon slices
1	small onion, minced
1½	cups light cream or milk
1	teaspoon salt, or more to taste
¼	cup pure maple syrup
¼	teaspoon cinnamon
	Sour cream, optional

1. Bring the sweet potatoes and water to a boil in a large, heavy-bottomed soup pot. Cover the pot, reduce the heat, and simmer for about 20 minutes, until the potatoes are very tender. Remove from the heat.

2. While the potatoes are cooking, sauté the bacon in a skillet, until crisp. Remove from the pan; blot with paper towels. Pour off all but about 3 tablespoons of fat, then add the onion and sauté for 5 minutes. Remove from the heat.

3. Working in batches, purée the potatoes and cooking water in a food processor or blender. (Always be careful when puréeing hot liquids in a blender. Never fill the container more than one-third full to avoid the risk of the lid blowing off.) Return the purée to the soup pot, then stir in the onion, light cream, salt, maple syrup, and cinnamon. Crumble the bacon and add that also. Heat, but do not boil, and serve piping hot. Put a small dollop of sour cream in each bowl, if desired.

Yield: 4–6 servings

CURRIED PUMPKIN-APPLE SOUP

Here's another recipe from Dianne Cutillo, who says her passion for maple syrup grew immensely while working on this book. Inspired by her new maple mania, she revised this recipe. More like "transformed," she reports. The maple mellows the curry, and together they accent pumpkin beautifully. Dianne's family and friends love the maple version. Why am I not surprised?

- **4 tablespoons butter**
- **1 cup chopped Vidalia onion**
- **1 small apple (Braeburn or Granny Smith), peeled, cored, and coarsely chopped**
- **2 cloves of garlic, crushed**
- **1 teaspoon curry powder**
- **½ teaspoon salt**
- **¼ teaspoon ground coriander**
- **⅛ teaspoon crushed red pepper**
- **2 cups chicken broth**
- **1 cup apple cider**
- **2 cups pumpkin purée**
- **1 cup light cream or half-and-half**
- **¼ cup pure maple syrup**

1. Melt the butter in a large saucepan over medium-high heat. Add the onion, apple, and garlic and sauté until soft, about 5 minutes. Add the curry powder, salt, coriander, and red pepper; cook for 1 minute.

2. Add the broth and cider and boil gently, uncovered, for 15 to 20 minutes.

3. Stir in the pumpkin, cream, and maple syrup; cook for 5 minutes.

4. Transfer the soup to a large pitcher. In a food processor or blender, purée the soup in three or four batches. Return the soup to the pot and cook over very low heat for 5 minutes; do not boil.

5. Ladle the soup into four bowls and serve piping hot.

Yield: 4 servings

CREAMY MAPLE FONDUE

Whether you serve this as a first course, on an hors d'oeuvres buffet, or for dessert, fondue is a delicious way to savor maple. It's another recipe from a member of the Citadelle Maple Syrup Producers' Cooperative in Quebec.

   ½ **cup pure maple syrup**
   2 **tablespoons cornstarch**
2½ **cups light cream or crème fraîche**
2–3 **cups firm fruits and berries, cut into small pieces**

1. Gently heat the maple syrup in a small saucepan for 5 minutes.

2. Mix the cornstarch with 2 tablespoons of the cream in a small bowl. Set aside.

3. In a medium-sized saucepan, bring the remaining cream to a simmer over medium heat; add the maple syrup. Whisk the cornstarch mixture into the cream mixture and cook, stirring continuously, until it comes to a boil. Boil while stirring for about 1 minute.

4. Serve the fondue in a small pan over a spirit lamp. Arrange the fruit and fondue forks or skewers around the fondue.

Yield: 4–6 servings

MAPLE-GLAZED CHICKEN WINGS

The chili sauce in this Citadelle marinade provides a nice contrast to the maple's sweetness. They're good out of the oven, but I also like them grilled (at medium-high heat, turning frequently, until thoroughly cooked).

  1   **small onion, chopped**
  ½   **cup pure maple syrup**
  5   **tablespoons chili sauce**
  2   **tablespoons cider vinegar**
  1   **tablespoon prepared mustard**
  1   **teaspoon Worcestershire sauce**
 2½   **pounds chicken wings (about 18)**

1. Combine the onion, maple syrup, chili sauce, vinegar, mustard, and Worcestershire sauce in a shallow dish.

2. Add the chicken wings to the dish, turn to coat, and marinate for at least 4 hours in the refrigerator, keeping them covered and turning occasionally. (The wings can be marinated for up to 2 days.)

3. Preheat oven to 400°F. Arrange the wings in a shallow baking pan so they are not touching one another. Discard remaining marinade.

4. Bake for 20 to 30 minutes, or until golden and crispy; turn the wings every 5 minutes to make sure they are browned evenly.

Yield: 4–6 appetizer servings

Free from Adulteration

MARY:
As you are going to town
Please send or bring some syrup down,
Some Maple Syrup and 'twill be
Bottled and labelled you will see.
JOHN:
Now, Mary, you don't want that stuff,
Of glucose we have had enough,
So this is what we'd better do,
Send to Vermont and get it new,
There, you know, laws are made,
Whereby adulterations are staid,
And if you doubt the label's true,
Why, testing it will prove to you
That in this State one can be sure
That he will get it clear and pure —
The other States no fines impose,
Perhaps 'tis pure, the maker knows!

— Vermont Maple Sugar Makers'
Association, 1894

ORANGE-MAPLE WINGS

Soaking chicken wings in this buttermilk-orange-maple bath makes the meat butter-tender and infuses it with sweetness. The flavor here is delicate and subtle, so serve them with buttered noodles or another simple side.

1½	**cups buttermilk**
⅓	**cup pure maple syrup**
2	**oranges, peeled and sectioned**
1	**teaspoon cinnamon**
2–2½	**pounds chicken wings (about 16–20)**

1. Mix the buttermilk and maple syrup in a large bowl.

2. Briefly process the orange sections and cinnamon in a food processor or blender to make a coarse purée.

3. Stir the orange mixture into the buttermilk, then add the chicken wings. Stir to coat. Cover and refrigerate for at least 1 hour or up to 24 hours, stirring every now and then.

4. Preheat oven to 400°F. Arrange the wings in a shallow baking pan so they are not touching one another.

5. Bake for 20 to 30 minutes, or until golden and crispy; turn the wings every 5 minutes to make sure they are evenly browned. Brush occasionally with some of the remaining marinade, but not in the last 5 minutes of cooking time.

Yield: 4–6 appetizer servings

Green Bean Salad

Cool, crisp, colorful — this is likely to become one of your most requested summer salads. It is best if the salad is left for at least an hour in the refrigerator before it is served.

- 3 cups fresh green beans, ends pinched off, and broken in half
- ½ cup Lemon-Basil Salad Dressing (page 60)
- 1 small red onion, halved and thinly sliced
- ½ cup finely chopped red bell pepper
- 1 rib of celery, finely chopped
- 1 tablespoon capers, optional but highly recommended

  Salt and freshly ground black pepper

1. Bring 2 quarts of salted water to a boil in a large pot. Add the beans and boil them, about 6 to 8 minutes, just until tender. Drain and transfer to a large bowl.

2. Immediately stir in the dressing, onion, bell pepper, celery, capers, if desired, and salt and pepper to taste. Cool thoroughly. Cover and refrigerate for at least 1 hour before serving.

Yield: 4 servings

The scarlet of the maples can shake me like a cry / Of bugles going by.

— William Bliss Carman

LEMON-BASIL SALAD DRESSING

Somebody could bottle this and make a fortune, that's how good it is. And it's very versatile. I use it on green salads, three-bean salads, and Green Bean Salad (page 59).

⅓ cup vegetable oil (may be part olive oil)
¼ cup apple cider vinegar
¼ cup pure maple syrup
1 tablespoon Dijon mustard
Salt and freshly ground black pepper
1½ teaspoons minced fresh basil or
½ teaspoon crushed dried basil
⅛ teaspoon finely grated lemon zest

1. Whisk together all the ingredients in a small bowl.

2. Taste, and adjust the flavor with a little more maple or vinegar, if needed. Bottle and refrigerate.

CREAMY LEMON-BASIL DRESSING

Prepare the dressing as above. Whisk in ½ to ¾ cup sour cream.

Yield: About 1 cup

ROASTED PEPPER AND CHICKPEA SALAD

The flavors of this salad create the nicest harmony. Do use smoked Cheddar — it combines nicely with the maple. Serve with grilled foods.

DRESSING
- ¼ cup vegetable oil
- Juice of 1 medium lemon (about 2 tablespoons)
- 2 tablespoons pure maple syrup
- 1½ tablespoons Dijon mustard

SALAD
- 3 large green or red bell peppers
- 2 cups cooked chickpeas (about 1 cup dried; rinsed and well-drained if using canned)
- 2 tablespoons minced onion
- ½ cup diced smoked Cheddar cheese
- ½ cup diced prosciutto or ham
- Salt and freshly ground black pepper

1. **TO MAKE THE DRESSING:** Whisk together the oil, lemon juice, maple syrup, and mustard in a large salad bowl. Set aside.

2. **TO MAKE THE SALAD:** Roast the whole peppers on a grill, over a hot burner, or under a broiler, turning often with tongs until the entire surface is charred. Put peppers into a plastic bag, twist shut, and freeze for 15 minutes — this will steam off the skins. Cut out the stem end, drain, and halve them. Remove the seeds and skins; the skins should peel off readily. Slice the peppers into narrow strips.

3. Toss the peppers into the dressing along with the chickpeas, onion, cheese, and prosciutto. Stir. Chill for several hours. Season to taste with salt and pepper before serving.

Yield: 4–5 servings

THE ROASTING DIFFERENCE

There was a time when I wouldn't bother with roasting peppers. When I actually did try it though, I was amazed at what a difference the roasting made in flavor and texture. In summer, I like to roast peppers on a hot grill; in other seasons, on top of the burner grid on my gas stove. You can also broil peppers in a shallow pan in any oven. For detailed instructions, see step 2 of this recipe.

Jícama, Grapes, and Orange Salad

Jícama (HEE-kah-mah) is one of those vegetables I'd never heard of when growing up. It looks something like a flattened potato, comes in a whole range of sizes, and is imported from Mexico. It's a bit plain, but adaptable, and it perks up in raw salads of this sort. Do let the salad sit in the refrigerator for a couple of hours before serving; bathing in the acid juices really helps the character of the jícama.

1	small jícama
	Juice of 2 medium limes (about 3 tablespoons)
2½	tablespoons pure maple syrup
1	tablespoon vegetable oil
	Pinch of salt
1	orange
½	cup green seedless grapes, halved
2	tablespoons minced red onion

1. Cut the jícama lengthwise into ¼-inch slabs and peel with a paring knife. Cut the slabs in ¼-inch-wide strips, then gather the strips and slice them into ¼-inch cubes. Put 1½ to 2 cups in a medium-sized bowl.

2. Pour the lime juice, maple syrup, and oil over the jícama; toss. Stir in the salt.

3. Halve the orange, remove any seeds, then free the sections with a knife. Squeeze them and their juices into the bowl, then add the grapes and onion. Cover and refrigerate for several hours before serving; stir once or twice while it's chilling.

Yield: 4–5 servings

CUCUMBER APPLE RAITA

This yogurt-based Indian dish is a cool, refreshing counterpoint to hot curries, though it could be served with any number of savory foods. There's an agreeable balance of sweet and sharp flavors, with the maple sounding a soft, background note. A pinch of chopped fresh mint really makes this shine, if you happen to have some on hand.

1	large cucumber, peeled, halved, and seeded
¼	teaspoon salt
1¼	cups plain yogurt
1½	tablespoons maple syrup
1	tablespoon minced onion
½	teaspoon finely grated orange zest
1	tart, firm apple, peeled, quartered, and cored

1. Chop the cucumber into uniform, small dice and transfer to a small bowl. Stir in the salt and set aside for 30 minutes.

2. Stir together the yogurt, maple syrup, onion, and orange zest. Chop the apple into uniform, small dice and stir into the yogurt. Cover and refrigerate for 30 minutes.

3. Squeeze the excess moisture out of the cucumber with your hands and fold the cucumbers into the yogurt mixture. Chill for at least 1 hour more, preferably longer, before serving.

Yield: 4–6 servings

MAPLE HISTORY

Legend in the United States has designated the first maple syrup maker and cook as an Iroquois woman, the wife of one Chief Woksis. One late-winter morning, the story goes, the chief headed out on one of his hunts, but not before yanking his tomahawk from the tree where he'd thrown it the night before. On this particular day the weather turned quite warm, causing the tree's sap to run and fill a container standing near the trunk. The woman spied the vessel and, thinking it was plain water, cooked her evening meal in it. The boiling that ensued turned the sap to syrup, flavoring the chief's meal as never before. And thus began the tradition of making maple syrup.

Thai-Inspired Mushroom Salad

Don't let the longish list of ingredients deter you: The need for the mushrooms to marinate in the refrigerator makes this a perfect do-ahead dish. And your taste buds will thank you.

- ¾ **pound white mushrooms**
- ½ **pound shiitake mushrooms**
- ½ **cup rice wine vinegar or rice vinegar**
- ¼ **cup orange juice**
- 3 **tablespoons pure maple syrup**
- 3 **tablespoons olive oil**
- 2 **tablespoons peanut butter**
- 2 **tablespoons tamari or soy sauce**
- 1 **tablespoon sesame oil**
- ¼ **teaspoon hot sauce (a mango-flavored one is nice)**
- 3 **scallions (2 optional)**
- 1 **clove of garlic, crushed**
- 1 **teaspoon grated ginger root**
- 1 **teaspoon finely minced lemongrass or lemon zest**
- 6 **cups (8 ounces) mesclun or baby spinach**
- ½ **medium red pepper, diced, optional**

1. Trim and slice the white mushrooms and put them in a large nonreactive bowl. Remove and discard the shiitake stems and slice the caps; add them to the bowl. Set aside.

2. Whisk together the vinegar, orange juice, maple syrup, olive oil, peanut butter, tamari, sesame oil, and hot sauce, in a medium-sized saucepan.

3. Finely mince one of the scallions; add to the vinegar mixture. Stir in the garlic, ginger root, and lemongrass.

4. Cook the mixture, stirring constantly, over low heat until it just comes to a simmer, about 5 minutes. Pour over the mushrooms; toss to coat. Cover and refrigerate for at least 3 hours or up to 3 days.

5. Divide the mesclun among six salad plates. Drain the mushrooms, then spoon them on top of the mesclun. Scatter the red pepper on the mushrooms, if desired. Slice the remaining two scallions diagonally into ½-inch pieces, if desired, and top the red pepper with them. Serve immediately.

Yield: 6 servings

CREAMY MAPLE SYRUP DRESSING

Because the ingredients for this dressing are kitchen staples in most homes, this is a great recipe for something special at the last minute. Created by the Ontario Maple Syrup Producers Association, it's just the right touch over butter lettuce or sliced fruit or berries.

- **1 cup mayonnaise**
- **½ cup pure maple syrup**
- **¼ cup apple cider vinegar**

1. Whisk together the mayonnaise, syrup, and vinegar in a small bowl until smooth.

2. Refrigerate, tightly covered, for at least 1 hour to let the flavors blend.

Yield: About 1½ cups

SALAD OILS

When making salad dressings, I call for vegetable oil and sometimes suggest that part olive oil is okay. Here's a place where your personal taste preferences come into play. Some people use only olive oil in salad dressings, but a good-quality extra-virgin olive oil with lots of fruity flavor can overpower other ingredients in a dressing, particularly a light maple syrup.

Canola, corn, peanut, safflower, soy, and sunflower oils are mild enough to let other flavors shine through.

MAPLE BALSAMIC DRESSING

Janice Wentworth of the Warren Farm & Sugarhouse in North Brookfield, Massachusetts, adapted this recipe from *Sweet Maple: Life, lore & recipes from the sugarbush*, which was copublished in 1993 by *Vermont Life* magazine and Chapters Publishing. The lime juice and cilantro give it the Southwestern flair that Jan's family loves. This dressing brings out the fruit flavor in any green salad with fruit in it.

> 3 **tablespoons balsamic vinegar**
> 2 **tablespoons pure maple syrup**
>   **Juice of 1 lime (about 1 tablespoon)**
> 1 **clove of garlic, minced**
> 1 **teaspoon finely chopped cilantro**
> 1 **teaspoon dry mustard**
> 1 **cup extra-virgin olive oil**
>   **Salt and freshly ground black pepper**

1. Combine the balsamic vinegar, maple syrup, lime juice, garlic, cilantro, and mustard in a food processor or blender.

2. With the motor running, slowly pour oil in through the feed tube until the dressing is emulsified. Add salt and pepper to taste.

3. Transfer to a bottle, cap, and refrigerate. The dressing may be stored for several weeks. Shake well before using.

Yield: About 1½ cups

Spicy Sweet & Sour Dressing

Just a little bit of this goes a long way to brighten up a tossed salad with an Asian accent. And this is the dressing of choice for the Sweet & Sour Chicken–Cashew Salad (page 87).

- ¼ **cup vegetable oil (part olive oil is good)**
- ¼ **cup apple cider vinegar**
- ¼ **cup pure maple syrup**
- 3 **tablespoons tamari or soy sauce**
- 1 **tablespoon Dijon mustard**
- 1 **clove of garlic, minced**
- ¼ **teaspoon finely grated orange zest**
- ⅛ **teaspoon cayenne**
- ⅛ **teaspoon ground cinnamon**
- ⅛ **teaspoon ground cloves**
- ⅛ **teaspoon ground ginger**

1. Combine all of the ingredients in a small bowl and whisk thoroughly. Taste and correct the precise balance of ingredients to your liking, adding a bit more vinegar, maple syrup, or spice, if you like.

2. Transfer to a bottle, cap, and refrigerate. Shake well before using.

Yield: About 1 cup

North Country Basting Sauce

Though not faithful to any particular school of thought on barbecue sauce, I can tell you that this barbecue sauce is versatile, spicy, and no slouch in the flavor department. It's tops on barbecued or broiled chicken. One thing I like to do with it is to combine it with hot peppers, more spices, and onions for the Hot & Spicy Shrimp and Sausage Kabobs (page 83).

 1 cup ketchup
⅔ cup apple cider vinegar
½ cup vegetable oil
½ cup pure maple syrup
 1 tablespoon Worcestershire sauce
 1 tablespoon Dijon mustard
½ teaspoon chili powder
½ teaspoon salt
¼ teaspoon cayenne pepper

1. Bring all of the ingredients to a boil in a small saucepan over medium heat, stirring occasionally. Reduce the heat and cook gently for 10 minutes, stirring from time to time.

2. Cool, then store in a covered jar in the refrigerator. This will keep for at least 4 weeks in the refrigerator in a tightly covered jar.

Yield: About 3 cups

Maple sugaring will not be hurried. It is more than the work of one night or one week; its rhythms are measured in sunlight and shadow, in the tilt of the earth's axis and in the ancient memories of trees.

— Will Weaver,
from the Foreword to
Sugartime by
Susan Carol Hauser

MAPLE-MUSTARD BARBECUE SAUCE

The Maine Maple Producers Association devised this recipe to inspire people to use maple syrup at meals other than breakfast. Simple, yummy, and makes enough for one chicken or pork tenderloin, or one batch of burgers — pass the barbecue sauce instead of ketchup.

⅓ cup pure maple syrup

2 tablespoons Dijon mustard, or other strong mustard

Juice of 1 medium lemon (about 2 tablespoons)

1 clove of garlic, crushed through a press

1 teaspoon cracked black pepper

½ teaspoon dried thyme leaves, crushed

⅓ cup peanut oil, or other mild oil

Basting Safety

Don't reuse marinade or sauce used on raw meat, poultry, or seafood unless it's boiled first to destroy any bacteria. If you're brushing sauce on food while it's grilling, don't do so during the last 5 minutes of cooking time. These food safety practices are recommended by the U.S. Department of Agriculture.

1. Whisk together the maple syrup, mustard, lemon juice, garlic, pepper, and thyme in a medium-sized bowl.

2. Slowly whisk in the oil to emulsify the sauce. Refrigerate, tightly covered, for up to several weeks.

Yield: ¾ cup

Maple-Basil Mustard

Not to blow my own horn, but my friend Dan says that his father — who collects mustards from all over the world — says this rivals the best of them. I know I sure like it, and I bet you will, too. It has guts, but with a pleasant, grainy personality. I use it on sandwiches, in salad dressings and marinades — with just about anything that calls for mustard.

⅓ **cup yellow mustard seeds**
2 **tablespoons dry mustard (I like Colman's)**
½ **cup water**
⅓ **cup apple cider vinegar**
⅓ **cup maple syrup**
¾ **teaspoon salt**
1 **teaspoon dried basil**

1. Put the mustard seeds, dry mustard, and water in a food processor or blender and process for 30 to 60 seconds, until the mixture takes on a thick, grainy texture. Scrape into a bowl and let sit, uncovered, for 2 hours or more; this helps release some of the bitter components.

2. After several hours, return the mixture to the food processor. Add the vinegar, maple syrup, salt, and basil and process until slightly smooth, yet still somewhat grainy.

3. Scrape into a double boiler and cook over simmering water for about 10 minutes, stirring often. Scrape into a bowl and let cool. Taste. It may need a touch more maple, or salt, or vinegar. Pack into a jar with a lid, then refrigerate; it will last indefinitely.

Yield: About 1½ cups

BEET AND PEAR RELISH

You can do all sorts or things with this sweet relish. In summer I like to serve it as is, on a plate with a variety of cold nibbles (try stirring in some fresh, chopped mint). In the cooler months I gently cook the whole shebang in a saucepan with a large handful of cranberries, until the cranberries pop and soften — maybe 10 minutes. This I serve with poultry or pork. Depending on how many cranberries you use, it might need a touch more maple to round off the tart edge. This keeps well in the refrigerator, tightly covered in a jar.

- 4 medium beets
- 1 firm, ripe pear, peeled, cored, and diced
- ⅓ cup chopped raisins
- 3 tablespoons pure maple syrup
  Juice of 1 lemon (about 2 tablespoons)
- 1 teaspoon minced fresh ginger root or
  ¼ teaspoon ground ginger
- ⅛ teaspoon cinnamon

1. Put the beets in a saucepan and add cold water to cover. Bring to a boil, then reduce the heat, cover the pan, and simmer until tender, about 30 minutes. Check for doneness by removing a beet and squeezing it quickly with your fingers; the beet will yield to the pressure when done. Drain the beets and run them under cold water.

2. When the beets are cool enough to handle, rub off the skins. Cut the beets into small dice.

3. Combine the beets, pear, raisins, maple syrup, lemon juice, ginger root, and cinnamon in a medium-sized bowl. Stir well. Refrigerate, covered, until serving.

Yield: About 2 cups

The first run, like first love, is always the best, always the fullest, always the sweetest.

— John Burroughs,
Winter Sunshine

Braised Onions with Bacon

I've really tried to like whole onions in the past but never really cared for any of the recipes I found. Until this one. This is nothing less than a sensational way to prepare boiled onions to serve with roasts, steak, and other meats. What you do is briefly sauté the onions in bacon fat, add water and seasonings, then cover and braise. Then you finish them with a touch of maple syrup and sprinkle on the bacon. Better to choose the medium boiling onions than the tiny ones — saves work in peeling.

1 pound medium boiling onions
3 bacon slices
½ cup water
1 teaspoon soy sauce
1 bay leaf
¼ teaspoon dried thyme
2 tablespoons pure maple syrup

1. Peel the onions and cut off the hairy part at the root end. Make a small shallow X in the root end, to encourage even cooking. Set aside.

2. Sauté the bacon until crisp in a heavy skillet. Using a slotted spoon or spatula, remove the bacon, blot with paper towels, and set aside. Add the onions to the fat and stir to coat. Cook over medium heat, partially covered, for 5 minutes, stirring occasionally.

3. Stir in the water, soy sauce, bay leaf, and thyme. Cover, reduce the heat slightly, and braise for 10 to 15 minutes, until the onions are almost tender all the way through. The exact cooking time will depend on the size of the onions.

4. Stir the maple syrup into the pan — which should still have a thin layer of liquid in it — and turn up the heat. Cook and stir, until the liquid turns to a syrupy glaze; it shouldn't take long. Crumble the bacon and stir it in. Remove the bay leaf. Serve hot, spooning on any available glaze.

VARIATION: You can make this a vegetarian dish by sautéeing the onions in olive oil instead of bacon fat. Garnish with seasoned croutons.

Yield: 4–5 servings

PINEAPPLE SALSA

Light and fruity, this salsa makes a great topping for grilled fish, chicken, or pork. Or dollop it on fresh greens for a tasty salad.

- **1 cup finely chopped fresh pineapple**
- **2 tablespoons finely minced red onion or scallion**
- **1 tablespoon chopped fresh cilantro or mint**
- **1 serrano pepper, seeded and finely minced**
  Juice of 1 small lime (about 1 tablespoon)
- **1 tablespoon pure maple syrup**

1. Combine all of the ingredients in a medium-sized bowl.

2. Refrigerate, covered, for at least 1 hour or up to 2 days.

Yield: About 1¼ cups

BOSTON BAKED BEANS

The mixture of beans, salt pork, molasses, and brown sugar popularly called *Boston baked beans* is said to be named after the tradition of Boston's Puritan women, who often prepared the dish for Saturday's supper, then served leftovers for breakfast the next morning because cooking on the Sabbath was forbidden. To make the meal authentic, add Steamed Brown Bread (page 78).

MAPLE BAKED BEANS

Baked beans, like chili, is one of those dishes that ignites controversy. Almost every variable can be debated. At the risk of adding fuel to the fire, here is my own favorite maple version.

1	**pound navy or pea beans**
⅓	**cup vegetable oil**
1	**cup chopped onions**
1	**green bell pepper, chopped**
1	**rib of celery, chopped**
2–3	**cloves of garlic, minced**
½	**cup pure maple syrup**
½	**cup tomato purée or crushed tomatoes**
2	**tablespoons blackstrap molasses**
2	**tablespoons apple cider vinegar**
1	**tablespoon Dijon mustard**
1½	**teaspoons salt**
¼	**teaspoon pepper**
1	**bay leaf**
¼	**cup chopped fresh parsley**

1. Pick the beans over, removing any rubble such as sticks and pebbles. Rinse them well, then place in a large bowl with plenty of hot water. Let soak for at least 1 hour, or as long as overnight. Drain, then combine the beans with about 4 quarts fresh hot water in a large pot. Bring to a boil and reduce the heat. Simmer, partially covered, just until tender — 1½ to 2 hours. Drain the beans, reserving the cooking water, into a large bowl.

2. While the beans cook, heat the oil in a large skillet. Add the onion, pepper, and celery and sauté for several minutes, adding the garlic at the end. Remove from the heat. Set aside. Preheat oven to 325°F.

3. Whisk together 1 cup of the reserved cooking water, the maple syrup, tomato purée, molasses, vinegar, mustard, salt, pepper, bay leaf, and parsley in a medium-sized bowl.

4. To the beans, add the sautéed vegetables and maple mixture; mix well. Pour the beans into a large, shallow casserole and cover tightly. Bake for 2½ to 3½ hours. Check periodically to make sure they have enough liquid, adding more of the reserved cooking water, if necessary.

Yield: About 6 servings

STUFFED SWEET POTATOES

Here's an easy, fun recipe, and a nice switch from candied sweet potatoes. I stuff only the best shells because I like the potatoes to be extra full.

> **4** medium sweet potatoes (about 2½ pounds)
> **¼** cup pure maple syrup
> **¼** cup sour cream
> **1** tablespoon butter
> **¼** teaspoon salt
>   Pinch of cinnamon
>   Pinch of nutmeg
>   Pinch of ground cloves
>   Brown sugar, optional

1. Preheat oven to 400°F. Prick the potatoes with a fork, once each, and bake on a baking sheet for 50 to 60 minutes, until the insides are soft. Remove from the oven and set aside until they are cool enough to handle.

2. Halve the potatoes lengthwise, carefully scoop out the insides, and reserve the shells. Combine the insides in a large bowl with the maple syrup, sour cream, butter, salt, spices, and brown sugar, if desired. Whip with an electric mixer until smooth. Pack the four best shells with the filling, mounding it in. Place close together in a pie plate or small casserole dish. Sprinkle the tops, if desired, with a touch of brown sugar. Bake for 20 to 25 minutes, until heated through.

Yield: 4 servings

Maple-Roasted Root Vegetables

Oven roasting seems to bring out the best in vegetables, especially these winter roots. The slow cooking in a mapley sauce fills the kitchen with mouthwatering aromas and produces one of my favorite down-home comfort foods.

3	medium carrots, peeled and cut into 1¼-inch chunks
3	medium parsnips, peeled and cut into 1¼-inch chunks
1	small (½ pound) yellow turnip
4	tablespoons butter
½	cup pure maple syrup
¼	cup bourbon or rum
1½	teaspoons kosher salt
	Freshly ground black pepper

1. Preheat oven to 350°F. Arrange the carrots, parsnips, and turnip in a single layer in a shallow roasting pan.

2. Heat the butter and maple syrup in a small saucepan just until the butter is melted, about 2 minutes. Remove from heat. Stir in the rum.

3. Pour the maple mixture over the vegetables and toss to thoroughly coat. Sprinkle the vegetables with the salt and pepper to taste.

4. Cover the pan with aluminum foil and bake for 25 minutes. Remove the pan from the oven, stir the vegetables, and bake, uncovered, until tender, 20 to 25 minutes longer.

Yield: 4 servings

Tom McCrumm

Tom McCrumm was not born to sugarmaking, he was called to it. It's become his profession and his passion. And he revels in sharing it.

When Tom was growing up, his family visited the Adirondacks, where they bought maple syrup at a farm. With eyes sparkling, he describes his lifelong fascination with a process where "you can take something that looks like water out of a tree and make something so good."

Later, he visited friends who boiled their own syrup, and while living on the West Virginia–Virginia border he made a gallon or two on his own. The mystery of sugaring brought him to Cornell University's maple research facility. Eventually, he bought South Face Farm in Ashfield, Massachusetts, where he collects sap from 4,000 to 4,500 taps. He's also executive director of the Massachusetts Maple Producers Association and grows and sells Christmas trees, all the while keeping his year-round maple mail-order business going.

Tom runs a restaurant at his sugarhouse on weekends during sugaring season; his wife, Judy Haupt, bakes the pies for the sugarhouse. The days often start at 5:30 A.M. and end toward midnight during the season, but Tom wouldn't have it any other way. At the sugarhouse, people waiting to get their fill of pancakes watch Tom boiling sap and ask questions. He says he "wants people to leave with a full brain and a full stomach," he talks about the science of production — such as indicators for the precise moment when the sap has become syrup: the right temperature and density to watch for so the syrup won't burn — and then he discusses the art: "You'll be boiling and, just like that, you see in one spot by the way it's boiling and the steam is rolling off that it's about to burn. You gain a feel for it." Tom's eyes are sparkling again. (His favorite recipe for Maple-Glazed Butternut Squash is on page 82.)

STEAMED BROWN BREAD

Traditionally this bread is made with molasses, not maple syrup; but once you've tasted this version, I think you'll excuse the liberties I've taken. Some folks don't like to tamper with tradition. I can remember publishing a recipe for Boston brown bread in a magazine, only to have some irate fellow write to the editor, blasting me for instructing readers to cut this with a sharp, serrated knife. Of course, the only correct way to slice it, this fellow maintained, was with twine — you wrap it around the loaf and pull the ends. Whether you use a knife, twine, or dental floss to slice it, do serve it with soft cream cheese. Some people like to soak the raisins in a little rum beforehand.

1 cup cornmeal
1 cup rye flour
1 cup whole-wheat flour
1 teaspoon baking powder
1 teaspoon baking soda
1 teaspoon salt
2 cups buttermilk
1 cup pure maple syrup
1 cup raisins

1. Grease two 13- or 16-ounce coffee cans, including the insides of their plastic lids. Place a trivet, large enough to support both cans, in the bottom of a wide, deep pot. Add hot water to about 3 inches above the trivet. Place the pot on a burner over medium heat.

2. Toss the cornmeal, rye and wheat flours, baking powder, baking soda, and salt to mix in a large bowl. In a separate bowl, beat the buttermilk and maple syrup.

3. Make a well in the dry ingredients, add the buttermilk mixture, and stir just to blend. Fold in the raisins.

4. Divide the batter evenly between the cans and put on the lids. Wrap a large piece of foil over each lid and secure with a heavy rubber band or twine. Using

a paring knife, poke a couple of steam vents in the foil. Put the cans in the water; the level should rise about half to two-thirds the way up the sides of the cans. Cover the pot with its lid if it will fit, or fashion a foil tent.

5. Bring the water to a boil. Reduce the heat and simmer for approximately 2 hours. Check the water level once or twice, and replenish with boiling water if it falls below the halfway mark. The bread is done when a tester inserted deeply into the center emerges clean. Remove the bread from the cans.

6. Preheat oven to 350°F and lightly grease a baking sheet. Place the breads on the prepared baking sheet and bake for 5 minutes to dry the outside surfaces. Serve warm, or transfer the bread to a wire rack to cool completely.

Yield: 2 round loaves, 8–10 slices each

Maple Syrup Production Statistics

With improved technology and increased demand for maple syrup and its related products, maple syrup production has grown dramatically during the past decade.

Sugarmaker and producer associations contribute both to the research efforts, by making grants to researchers, and to the increased demand, through concerted and coordinated marketing efforts.

While Vermont maintains its place as the largest U.S. producer, Quebec is now the world leader. See at right how the states and provinces stacked up in 2000.

STATE/PROVINCE	GALLONS
Quebec	7,470,000
Vermont	460,000
Ontario	445,000
Maine	250,000
New York	210,000
New Brunswick	90,000
Wisconsin	65,000
New Hampshire	75,000
Pennsylvania	47,000
Michigan	44,000
Massachusetts	39,000
Ohio	34,000
Connecticut	7,000

WHOLE-WHEAT AND OAT YEAST LOAVES OR ROLLS

It takes a considerable amount of maple syrup to get any kind of clear maple flavor from a yeast bread. I do have a trick, however, for accenting the maple flavor when I use this recipe to make rolls, as I often do. What I do is brush the rolls after they have risen with a mixture of 1 tablespoon melted butter and 1 tablespoon maple syrup, which not only clarifies the maple flavor but gives the rolls a dark, glossy sheen. Don't do this on the large loaves, however, because the tops will burn during the longer baking time. This makes an excellent toasting loaf.

1¼	cups milk
¾	cup buttermilk
¾	cup old-fashioned oats
⅓	cup warm (105°F to 115°F) water
1	tablespoon active dry yeast
3½	cups whole-wheat flour
5	tablespoons butter, softened
⅔	cup pure maple syrup
1	egg, lightly beaten
1	tablespoon salt
3	cups unbleached or all-purpose flour (approximately)

1. Lightly oil a large bowl. Set aside.

2. Warm the milk and buttermilk in a saucepan until hot to the touch. Put the oats in a large bowl and pour the warm milk over them. Set aside.

3. Pour the water into a separate, small bowl and sprinkle on the yeast. When the oat liquid cools to about body temperature, stir in the dissolved yeast. Using a heavy wooden spoon, stir 2 cups of the whole-wheat flour into the liquid, beating hard for 1 minute. Cover this "sponge" and let rise for 1 hour.

4. Beat the soft butter into the sponge, followed by the maple syrup, egg, and salt. Stir in the remaining 1½ cups whole-wheat flour. Cover and let rise for 10 minutes.

5. Now start stirring in the unbleached flour, about ½ cup at a time, until the dough becomes too stiff to beat. Then turn the dough onto a floured surface. Begin kneading, gently at first, using flour as needed to prevent sticking. Knead a good 10 minutes, until the dough is smooth and fairly elastic. Place in the oiled bowl and turn to coat the entire surface. Cover, and let rise until double in bulk, about 1 hour.

6. Grease 2 large loaf pans. Punch the dough down, knead briefly, and divide it in half. Shape the dough into loaves and place the loaves in the prepared pans. (I like to roll it out into a tapered rectangle, the taper toward me, and roll up the dough like a carpet; this puts adequate tension on the dough and gives the top a nice, rounded appearance.)

7. Cover and set aside, to double in bulk, 30 to 45 minutes. Preheat oven to 375°F when the loaves are almost doubled.

8. When fully doubled, bake the loaves for about 45 minutes, until nicely browned. Remove the loaves from their pans and cool on a rack. Store in plastic bags.

Note: To make dinner rolls, break off golf ball–sized pieces of dough and shape into rounds. Place, almost touching, on a buttered baking sheet. Let rise, brush with glaze (see recipe introduction), and bake for 25 to 30 minutes.

Yield: 2 large loaves; 2 dozen rolls

Maple-Glazed Butternut Squash

Tom McCrumm of South Face Farm in Ashfield, Massachusetts, executive director of the Massachusetts Maple Producers Association, says he is not a fan of butternut squash. Unless, of course, it's glazed with maple syrup seasoned by the subtle nutmeg flavor of mace, as in this recipe created by Tom's wife, Judy Haupt.

- **1 medium butternut squash (about 1½ pounds)**
- **⅔ cup water**
- **¼ cup pure maple syrup**
- **¼ cup dark rum**
- **¼ teaspoon ground mace**

1. Peel, seed, and quarter the squash. Cut, crosswise, into ½-inch slices to make about 5½ cups.

2. Bring the squash, water, maple syrup, rum, and mace to a boil in a large saucepan over medium-high heat. Reduce the heat and simmer, covered, for 15 minutes, or until the squash is tender. While the squash is simmering, warm a serving dish in a 200°F oven or by filling it with very hot water.

3. Reserving the cooking liquid, transfer the squash with a slotted spoon to the warmed serving dish.

4. Increase the heat and boil the cooking liquid about 3 minutes, or until it is thickened. Pour the thickened liquid over the squash.

Yield: 4 servings

Hot & Spicy Shrimp and Sausage Kabobs

Whether or not you agree with my friend Cindy — who called this the best meal of her entire life (she had a sheltered childhood) — I do think you'll be pleased. The heat can be regulated here by gauging the amount and type of chili peppers you use; for most folks, I find the 2 tablespoons of jalapeños sufficient. Of course, if you have a stash of fresh, hot peppers you fancy, then use them instead. Good beer-drinking grub this is. But if you're limiting your meat consumption, skewer up 2 pounds of shrimp and skip the sausage.

1¼ cups North Country Basting Sauce (page 68)
    Juice of ½ medium lemon (about
    1½ tablespoons)
2   tablespoons minced onion
2   tablespoons minced jalapeño peppers,
    canned or fresh
1   pound chorizo or linguiça sausage
1   pound fresh large shrimp in the shell

1. Blend the basting sauce, lemon juice, onion, and jalapeño peppers in a large bowl. Set aside.

2. Bring 2 quarts of water to a boil in a large pot. Prick the sausage several times with a fork and then boil for 5 minutes. When cool enough to handle, cut into ½-inch slices and add to the marinade along with the shrimp. Stir to coat well. Cover and set aside for 1 hour; it may be refrigerated for several hours.

3. Preheat the grill to medium-high. Thread four or five long skewers alternately with the shrimp and sausage. Either grill or broil, far enough from the heat to prevent charring, for about 10 minutes total or until the shrimp are pink. Turn occasionally during cooking and brush with more sauce. And be sure to tell your guests that the shrimp is in the shell.

Yield: 4 servings

SPICY SAUSAGE

Highly seasoned, chorizo and linguiça make a delicious addition to casseroles, soups, stews, and pizza, as well as kabobs.

Chorizo. Flavored with garlic, chili powder, and other spices, chorizo is used in both Mexican and Spanish cooking. The Mexican version is made with fresh ground pork, while the Spaniards use smoked pork. It's also used to fill enchiladas.

Linguiça. A Portuguese specialty, this sausage is heavily garlic-flavored and used in Latin dishes.

Roast Breast of Chicken with Red Wine–Blueberry Glaze

The Shakers applied the virtues of simplicity, purity, and perfection to their work and to themselves. For their cooking, that meant fresh ingredients, simply prepared, as in this wonderful dish from James Haller and Jeffrey Paige's *Cooking in the Shaker Spirit*, which, alas, is no longer in print.

Red Wine–Blueberry Glaze
- 1 pint fresh blueberries, picked over and washed
- 1 cup red wine
- 1 cup pure maple syrup
- ¼ cup Dijon mustard

Roast Chicken
- 4 bone-in chicken breasts (1 pound each)
- 4 tablespoons chopped fresh parsley
- Salt and freshly ground black pepper
- Paprika
- Garlic powder

1. Bring the blueberries, wine, maple syrup, and mustard to a boil in a medium saucepan. Reduce heat to low and simmer until reduced by one-third, about 1 hour 15 minutes.

2. **To roast the chicken:** Preheat oven to 400°F. Rinse the chicken breasts under cold water and pat dry. Split the chicken breasts in half.

3. Place the chicken in a roasting pan and sprinkle with the parsley and as much salt, pepper, paprika, and garlic as you like. Roast the chicken for 30 minutes.

4. Remove the chicken from the oven and spread with the glaze. Return to the oven and cook for 10 minutes longer, or until the meat is tender and the juices run clear when the meat is pierced with a fork.

Yield: 8 servings

SALMON WITH MANGO SALSA

Salmon certainly doesn't need much adornment, but a sauce or a salsa just seems to bring out the flavor of the fish. When I'm planning what to dress it up with, I'm torn between a simple Maple Glaze (page 89), Pineapple Salsa (page 73), or Mango Salsa. Sometimes I just let the greengrocer decide: If there isn't a beautiful, ripe pineapple or mango, it's the glaze. If both are available, well, sometimes I make two kinds of salsa and eat the fish with a little bit of each.

MANGO SALSA
- 1 ripe mango, peeled, pitted, and chopped
- 1 small jalapeño pepper, seeded and finely chopped
- 2 scallions, green part only, finely chopped
  Juice of 1 small lime (about 1 tablespoon)
- 1 tablespoon pure maple syrup

SALMON
- 4 salmon fillets or steaks (6–8 ounces each)
  Juice of 1 small lime (about 1 tablespoon)
- 1 tablespoon pure maple syrup

1. **TO MAKE THE SALSA:** Combine the mango, jalapeño, scallion, lime juice, and maple syrup in a small bowl. Refrigerate, covered, to allow the flavors to blend. (The salsa will keep for up to 2 days, refrigerated.)

2. **FOR THE SALMON:** Preheat the grill to medium-high (or preheat the broiler).

3. Whisk together the lime juice and maple syrup. Set aside.

4. Grill the salmon (or broil 4 inches from the heat; skin side down if using fillets) for 4 minutes, turn, and brush the maple mixture onto the fish. Grill 2 to 3 minutes longer, or until cooked through. Salmon steaks require 2 to 3 additional minutes of cooking time.

5. Transfer salmon to a platter or dinner plates, spoon the salsa over it, and serve.

Yield: 4 servings

It is said that children have often grown up in this county without tasting any but maple sugar.

— Susan Fenimore Cooper,
Rural Hours, 1850

CHICKEN WITH MAPLE-MUSTARD GLAZE

This recipe is an adaptation of one developed by my late friend Richard Sax, who was a gifted cook, food writer, and all-around fine person. What he would do is make the sauce, minus the mustard, and brush it on the chicken. Then he would broil the chicken 6 inches from the heat, 15 minutes on each side, and brush the mustard on at the last minute. Here's my way, for the grill, but you could also broil it Richard's way.

- 1 broiler-fryer chicken (2½–3 pounds), cut up
- ¼ cup pure maple syrup
- 3 tablespoons Dijon mustard
- 2 teaspoons tamari or soy sauce
  Juice of ½ small lemon (about 1 tablespoon)
- 1 clove of garlic, minced
- ½ teaspoon freshly ground black pepper

1. Trim the excess fat from the chicken. Rinse the chicken under cold water and blot dry with paper towels. Place the chicken in a large, shallow casserole dish and set aside.

2. Combine the maple syrup, mustard, tamari, lemon juice, garlic, and pepper in a small saucepan; bring to a boil. Boil for 1 minute. Remove from the heat.

3. Brush the chicken on both sides with half the maple sauce. Refrigerate for 30 to 60 minutes.

4. Preheat the grill to medium-high. Grill, periodically turning and basting the chicken pieces with the remaining sauce, until the meat is tender and the juices run clear when meat is pierced with a fork, about 15 minutes per side. Total cooking time will vary depending on the size of the pieces being cooked.

Yield: 4 servings

Sweet & Sour Chicken–Cashew Salad

This is not so much the sort of chicken salad you'd put in a sandwich as it is something you'd arrange in the middle of a colorful plate of greens and serve for a light lunch or dinner. There are all sorts of contrasting flavors and textures here, much to the salad's advantage.

½ cup Spicy Sweet & Sour Dressing (page 67)
2 tablespoons tahini
2 cups bite-sized chunks cooked chicken
1 rib of celery, finely chopped
2 scallions, thinly sliced
½ cup coarsely chopped cashews
1 tablespoon minced jalapeño peppers, optional
   Fresh lemon juice
   Salt and freshly ground black pepper
   Greens
   Minced raisins, optional

1. Put the salad dressing into a large bowl and thoroughly whisk in the tahini so the mixture thickens a little. Fold in the chicken, celery, scallions, cashews, and peppers, if desired.

2. Squeeze in a little lemon juice and sprinkle in salt and pepper, then taste and adjust the seasonings to your liking. Cover and refrigerate until serving. Serve on a plate of greens, garnished very lightly with the raisins, if desired.

Yield: 4 servings

Flavor Options

Tahini, a sesame seed paste, is widely available in health food stores and many larger supermarkets. But you can vary the flavor of the chicken salad by skipping the tahini and substituting peanut butter or about a tablespoon of Dijon mustard.

Four-Bean Bake with Hamburger

Visitors to the Sugarbush Maple Syrup Festival at the Kortright Centre for Conservation in Woodbridge, Ontario, get a bonus with the guide they use to take a self-guided tour of the bush: maple recipes, including this one for a casserole that would travel well to a sugaring-off party or another potluck event.

- 8 ounces lean ground beef
- ½ cup chopped onion
- 2 cups baked beans (one 16-ounce can)
- 1 cup canned cannelini beans, rinsed and drained
- 1 cup canned pinto beans, rinsed and drained
- 1 cup canned red kidney beans, rinsed and drained
- 6 tablespoons barbecue sauce
- 6 tablespoons pure maple syrup
- 3 teaspoons prepared mustard
  Salt and freshly ground black pepper

1. Preheat oven to 400°F. Sauté the ground beef and the onion in a large heavy skillet for 4 to 5 minutes over medium-high heat.

2. Stir in the baked beans, cannelini beans, pinto beans, kidney beans, barbecue sauce, maple syrup, and mustard. Add salt and pepper to taste. Bring the mixture to a boil.

3. Transfer the mixture to a Dutch oven or casserole dish and bake for 20 to 30 minutes, stirring occasionally, until bubbly.

Yield: 4 servings

MAPLE BEEF TERIYAKI

Ilona Sherratt, the illustration coordinator at Storey Books, was creating art for the revision of this book around the same time she was asked to prepare food for a party. Her natural love of real maple syrup inspired her to use it as the base for this beef teriyaki. It was such a huge hit that my editor requested that I include the recipe in the new edition. And so I did.

- ¼ **cup pure maple syrup**
- ¼ **cup tamari or soy sauce**
- 2 **tablespoons vegetable oil**
- 2 **tablespoons sesame oil**
- 1 **tablespoon five-spice powder**
- 2 **pounds lean beef, sliced across the grain into ¼-inch strips**

1. Mix the maple syrup, tamari, vegetable oil, sesame oil, and five-spice powder in a large nonreactive bowl. Add the beef and toss well to coat the meat.

2. Cover and refrigerate overnight; stir occasionally.

3. Prepare a grill or broiler for medium-high heat.

4. Drain the beef and pat dry with paper towels. Thread the meat onto eight long or sixteen short skewers (if using wooden skewers, soak them in water for 30 minutes before threading on the beef).

5. Grill or broil the beef until tender, turning occasionally, about 6 minutes total for medium rare.

Yield: 8 main-course or 16 appetizer servings

Maple Glaze

When I eat breakfast out, it never ceases to amaze me how many people dip bacon, ham, or sausage into the maple syrup on the plate from their pancakes, waffles, or French toast.

Maple does have a have a way of bringing out the best in meats. To enhance the experience, add a few ingredients to maple syrup and you'll have a delicious glaze for a variety of meats, from ham, whole or in steaks, to pork tenderloin and chicken or turkey.

Just combine ¾ cup pure maple syrup, ¼ cup apple cider vinegar, 1 teaspoon dry mustard, and a pinch of ground cloves in a small saucepan. Bring the mixture to a boil. If you want to glaze meat while it's still roasting in the oven, boil the mixture for a minute or two, because it will thicken further in the oven. If you want to serve the glaze as a sauce, boil it for 3 to 5 minutes so it will thicken.

Be creative with your glaze: Use plum jam or soy sauce instead of the vinegar, or prepared Dijon mustard instead of the dry mustard.

Kortright Centre
for Conservation

Just about every sugarmaker has had to boil sap through the night at least once. Visitors to the Kortright Centre for Conservation in Woodbridge, Ontario, get a feel for that ritual in a "Maple Syrup by Lantern" hike through Kortright's sugarbush. The event, in its third year, also includes a dinner featuring a maple syrup buffet and has sold out for the past two years.

"We've had a lot of disappointed people," said Wendy Heron, special events coordinator at Kortright. The sugarbush is part of Kortright's 800 acres of green space, where the Toronto and Region Conservation Authority provides environmental learning opportunities.

But during Kortright's six-week Sugarbush Maple Syrup Festival visitors can take self-guided tours of the sugarbush. Visitors see the history and the process of sugarmaking on the walk. One display shows the gash in the tree and the twig, inserted into the cut, that allows sap to run into a birch bark container, which Natives would have used to collect sap. Another exhibit is of a modern gravity-fed tube system. There's a pioneer sugar camp set up as one would have been in the nineteenth century and a modern sugar shack that houses an evaporator.

"People enjoy trying on the wooden yoke and two buckets that were used to carry sap from the trees to the sugarhouse, and getting samples of sap and syrup so they can taste the difference," Wendy said.

They can also eat pancakes at the Visitor Centre, and, if they were enraptured by the magic of making maple syrup, they can buy a do-it-yourself syrup-making kit. (Kortight's recipe for Four-Bean Bake with Hamburger is on page 88.)

CRISPY MAPLE SPARERIBS

All you need to make a meal of these is a big green salad — and plenty of napkins.

3	pounds lean pork spareribs
1	small onion, finely chopped
¾	cup pure maple syrup
1	tablespoon chili sauce
1	tablespoon red wine vinegar
1	tablespoon Worcestershire sauce
¼	teaspoon dry mustard
	Salt and freshly ground black pepper

1. Preheat oven to 400°F. Arrange the ribs on a wire rack in a roasting pan and roast for 30 minutes.

2. Combine the onion, maple syrup, chili sauce, vinegar, Worcestershire, mustard, and salt and pepper to taste in a small saucepan and bring to a boil; boil for 5 minutes.

3. Reduce oven to 350°F. Remove the ribs from the rack and arrange in a baking pan; brush them with the sauce. Bake uncovered for 45 to 60 minutes, basting frequently, until ribs are glazed to a deep mahogany color.

4. Cut between the rib bones with a sharp knife and serve.

Yield: 4 servings

Pork Magic

Pork and maple is my favorite combination, at least I think so until I think about seafood and maple, poultry and maple, or, well, anything and maple. It's especially easy to indulge in pork and maple with the wider availability of so-tender-you-can-cut-it-with-a-fork pork tenderloins.

For a quick meal, cut the tenderloin crosswise into 1-inch slices, pound them into ¼-inch medallions, and sprinkle them with dried sage or rosemary. Dredge lightly in flour if desired, and sauté in a little butter and olive oil. Serve with warm maple syrup, or a sauce of maple syrup and melted crabapple jelly, for dipping.

It takes little imagination to vary the dish: add chopped fresh ginger root when you cook the meat; sprinkle dried cranberries or toasted nuts over the medallions before serving; or top with fruit salsa.

MAPLE VINEGAR–ROASTED PORK

John Boyajian tells a great and colorful tale about the serendipitous path that took him from graduate school studies in education to the food business — from importing caviar and smoked salmon to producing top-quality flavored oils and vinegars. His recipe for pork tenderloin gets maple flavor from his maple vinegar, and its lovely touch of herb from his oil infused with rosemary.

½ cup rosemary oil
¼ cup maple vinegar (Sources, page 132)
3 cloves of garlic, finely chopped
1 tablespoon Dijon mustard
1 tablespoon honey
2 pork tenderloins (12 ounces each)
   Salt and freshly ground black pepper
   Cranberry or other chutney, optional

1. Combine the rosemary oil, maple vinegar, garlic, mustard, and maple syrup in a large nonreactive bowl. Add the pork and turn to coat with the marinade. Cover and refrigerate for 8 hours or overnight, turning and basting the pork a few times.

2. Preheat oven to 375°F. Drain the pork, discarding the excess marinade. Place the pork in a roasting pan and season with salt and pepper.

3. Roast for 20 to 30 minutes, or until an instant-read or meat thermometer inserted into the center of the tenderloins registers 155°F. Remove from oven and let stand for 15 minutes. (The tenderloins may also be grilled over medium heat for approximately 10 minutes per side.)

4. Slice thinly and serve with cranberry chutney, if desired.

Yield: 4 servings

HAM STEAK IN RUM-RAISIN SAUCE

Here's a simple tasty way to prepare ham steaks. Try this with biscuits and Braised Onions with Bacon (page 72.)

1	pound ham steak
1	cup apple cider
¼	cup plus 2 tablespoons pure maple syrup
¼	cup dark rum
2–3	tablespoons orange juice, preferably fresh
½	cup raisins

1. Preheat oven to 350°F. Put the ham steak in a shallow casserole dish slightly larger than the steak. Set aside.

2. Bring the cider, ¼ cup of the maple syrup, the rum, orange juice, and raisins to a near boil in a small saucepan. Cover and let sit for 10 minutes. Remove the raisins with a slotted spoon, put them in a small bowl, and spoon enough of the hot liquid over them to cover completely. Pour the remaining liquid over the ham and bake for 1 hour.

3. When the hour is up, remove the ham from the oven and preheat the broiler.

4. Combine the raisins and their soaking liquid in a food processor or blender with several tablespoons of the casserole juice and the remaining 2 tablespoons maple syrup. Process briefly — a little roughness is good — and pour it directly over the ham. Place the ham under the broiler for just a few moments, until it sizzles and browns; keep a close eye on it. Serve hot.

Yield: 2–3 servings

There's no finer sight or smell in Spring than steam billowing from a sugar shack.

— Charlie Tetreault,
Log Cabin Chronicles

GINGERED PORK MEDALLIONS

A quick skillet recipe, this dish with Asian flavors can be made with pork tenderloins, cut crosswise into ½-inch thick pieces then pounded as described below, or boneless chicken breasts. Serve it with rice and a salad of snow peas and radishes with an orange vinaigrette.

4	boneless pork chops, ¾-inch each
⅓	cup all-purpose flour
½	teaspoon salt
¼	teaspoon freshly ground black pepper
2	tablespoons butter
2	shallots, thinly sliced
1	tablespoon peeled and finely chopped fresh ginger root
1	clove of garlic, finely chopped
½	cup dry white wine or chicken broth
¼	cup pure maple syrup
¼	cup teriyaki sauce
2	tablespoons rice vinegar

1. Using a meat mallet or rolling pin, flatten the pork chops between sheets of waxed paper or plastic wrap to a thickness of about ¼ inch.

2. Combine the flour, salt, and pepper in a shallow dish. Melt 1 tablepoon of the butter in a heavy large skillet over medium-high heat. Dredge the pork in the flour mixture, shaking off the excess. Add half of the pork to the skillet and sauté until brown and cooked through, about 2 minutes per side. Transfer to a platter and keep warm by covering loosely with foil. Repeat with remaining pork and butter.

3. Reduce heat to medium. Add the shallot, ginger root, and garlic to the pan and sauté for 2 minutes. Stir in the wine, maple syrup, teriyaki, and vinegar. Cook, uncovered, for 5 to 7 minutes, stirring occasionally, until the sauce thickens slightly. Return the pork to the pan and heat through.

Yield: 4 servings

CHAPTER FOUR

Maple Sweets

In this chapter, you'll find a heavenly assortment of treats that explore and exploit the sweetening power and delectable flavor of maple. Pile almond or chocolate bar cookies on a platter or fill your cookie jar with spicy or gingery gems. Or delight your family with the mouthwatering odors of maple pies and cakes baking in the oven, the creamy goodness of maple-inspired ice cream, or a maple-infused coffee shake.

SUGAR ON SNOW

There is nothing more authentically traditional among sugarmakers than a springtime Sugar-on-Snow party. It is actually an easy-to-make treat year round, according to the Vermont Maple Sugar Makers' Association/ Vermont Maple Promotion Board, which distributes these guidelines. Sugar on Snow is traditionally served with sour pickles and plain doughnuts to cut the sweetness of the candy.

- 1 quart pure maple syrup
- 1 cup (2 sticks) butter
- 1 tub of packed snow or well-crushed ice (size depends on number being served — can be as small as a quart, but increase accordingly)

1. Heat the syrup and butter in a large pot over medium heat, watching carefully; turn the heat down if it threatens to boil over.

2. When a candy thermometer reaches 234°F, cool slightly and test by spooning a tablespoon of syrup over the snow. If the syrup sits on top of the snow and clings to a fork like taffy, it's ready.

3. Pour in "ribbons" over snow or ice packed in bowls.

Yield: Varies

Grandma stood by the brass kettle and with the big wooden spoon she poured hot syrup on each plate of snow. It cooled into soft candy, and as fast as it cooled, they ate it. They could eat all they wanted, for maple sugar never hurt anybody.

— Laura Ingalls Wilder,
*Little House
in the Big Woods*

GORP BARS

Good Old Raisins and Peanuts bars. Moist and chewy, they travel well and are great for brown baggers and hikers.

    1   cup unsalted, unsweetened peanut butter
        (smooth or crunchy)
    ½   cup (1 stick) butter, softened
    1   cup pure maple syrup
    1   egg
    1   teaspoon pure vanilla extract
    ½   teaspoon baking soda
    1   cup old-fashioned oats
    1   cup whole-wheat or unbleached flour
    1½ cups finely chopped, raw unsalted peanuts
    1½ cups raisins or dried cranberries

1. Preheat oven to 350°F. Grease a 9- by 13-inch baking pan and set it aside.

2. Cream the peanut butter and butter with an electric mixer. Gradually add the maple syrup, egg, vanilla, and baking soda. Stir in the oats and flour, just to blend, followed by the peanuts and raisins. Using floured hands, pat the mixture evenly into the prepared pan.

3. Bake for about 30 minutes, just until the edges begin to brown. Cool on a wire rack before cutting into bars.

Yield: About 2 dozen bars

Beyond Syrup: Maple Products

Besides maple syrup and maple sugar, there are several other traditional products made and sold by sugarmakers.

Maple Cream. Also called *maple butter,* this is produced by heating maple syrup, cooling it, then stirring until a creamy thick consistency is reached. It's excellent on toast, bagels, doughnuts, and more, and is used as a cake frosting.

Maple Candy. For candies, the syrup is cooked about 10°F hotter than for maple cream, then poured into molds.

Maple Sugar. Made by continuing to boil down syrup — past the candy stage — until crystallization takes place.

Maple Vinegar. Wonderful for marinades and deglazing pans, maple vinegar was traditionally made with sap from the very end of the sugaring season. Syrup made from that sap contains metabolites, nutrients that will feed the leaf buds, and has off-flavors that are not desirable for retail sales.

DREAMY ALMOND BARS

Warning: You could easily put on several pounds just *reading* this recipe, let alone eating it. These bars are entirely out of the question if you value your waistline. On the other hand, this is a large recipe, to be cut into small pieces, so you could stash away a piece or two for yourself and put out the rest for a Christmas or New Year's gathering. I specify a 10- by 15-inch jelly-roll pan, but I have actually used an 11- by 17-inch pan. It's not a difficult recipe, but you should read the instructions through before starting, just to be sure of the technique.

CRUST

- 1   cup (2 sticks) butter, softened
- ½   cup firmly packed brown sugar
- 1   egg, at room temperature
- 3   cups unbleached or all-purpose flour

TOPPING
- ½   cup (1 stick) butter
- ¾   cup pure maple syrup
- ½   cup firmly packed brown sugar
- ¼   cup honey
- ¼   cup heavy cream
- 2   cups chopped almonds
- 1   teaspoon pure vanilla extract

1. **TO MAKE THE CRUST:** Lightly grease a 10- by 15-inch jelly-roll pan and set aside. Preheat oven to 375°F.

2. Cream the butter and sugar in a large bowl. When light, beat in the egg. Add the flour, about ½ cup at a time, working it in with a wooden spoon. Divide the dough into four pieces and put a piece in each quadrant of the jelly-roll pan.

3. Push the dough into the pan with floured hands, forming a seamless crust. Keep it as even as you can and work it up the sides to the top of the rim. It won't look perfect, but just do the best job you can; if you want to flatten it out some,

roll it with a pin. Cover with plastic and chill for 15 minutes. Poke the dough three or four times with a fork, then bake for 15 minutes. Cool on a wire rack. Mix a tiny amount of flour and water together to make a thick paste, and rub a little into the fork holes to close them up.

4. TO MAKE THE TOPPING: After the crust has cooled for about 20 minutes, melt the butter in a large saucepan. Add the maple syrup, brown sugar, and honey and bring to a boil. When it boils, add the cream and bring back to a boil. Boil for 2 minutes. Quickly remove from heat and stir in the almonds and vanilla. Spread evenly over the crust and bake for 20 minutes; it will bubble and darken somewhat. Cool thoroughly on a wire rack, then cut into bars.

Yield: 2–3 dozen bars

RICH MAPLE SHORT CRUST

This is a good, maple-laced cookie bar crust that's a cinch to prepare. I use it, among other things, for Black-Bottom Cheesecake Bars (page 100).

¾ **cup (1½ sticks) butter, softened**
⅓ **cup pure maple syrup, at room temperature**
½ **teaspoon pure vanilla extract**
 2 **cups unbleached or all-purpose flour**
½ **teaspoon salt**

1. Cream the butter with an electric mixer in a medium-sized bowl. Continue to beat, gradually adding the maple syrup and vanilla. Combine the flour and salt, then gradually add to the creamed mixture, working it in with a wooden spoon.

2. Using floured hands, pat evenly into a 9- by 13-inch baking pan; roll with a can or bottle to even it out. Cover, then refrigerate until needed.

Yield: 9- by 13-inch crust

Black-Bottom Cheesecake Bars

I don't mix chocolate with maple syrup too often, because chocolate tends to overpower the subtle taste of maple. When I do, though — such as in these scrumptious cheesecake bars — I really like to go all out. I find that since the chocolate ends up underneath, you can still appreciate the maple-flavored cheese layer. These are excellent.

1	recipe Rich Maple Short Crust (page 99)
1	pound cream cheese, softened
½	cup sour cream, at room temperature
2	eggs, at room temperature
¾	cup pure maple syrup, at room temperature
1	teaspoon pure vanilla extract
1	teaspoon fresh lemon juice (from half of a small lemon)
1½–2	cups semisweet chocolate chips

1. Prepare the short crust as directed and spread in a 9- by 13-inch pan. Preheat oven to 400°F.

2. Using an electric mixer, beat the cream cheese until fairly light textured. Beat in the sour cream and then the eggs, one at a time. Gradually beat in the maple syrup, followed by the vanilla and lemon juice.

3. Sprinkle the chocolate chips evenly over the crust. Slowly pour on the cheese mixture. Bake for 15 minutes, then reduce oven to 350°F and bake for 30 minutes longer. The cake will be puffy and probably will have developed cracks on the top.

4. Cool on a wire rack, cover, then chill before cutting into bars.

Yield: About 2 dozen bars

COFFEE CHIP COOKIES

This is a classic chocolate chip cookie recipe from my original self-published maple book. It incorporates almost all of my gustatory weaknesses — butter, maple, coffee, chocolate, and walnuts — and, I suspect, accounts for no small share of my dentist's annual income. Dedicated to my friend Cindy, who'll take her coffee any way she can.

- 1 cup (2 sticks) butter, softened
- 1 cup pure maple syrup, at room temperature
- 1½ tablespoons instant espresso powder or instant coffee
- 2 tablespoons hot water
- 2 teaspoons pure vanilla extract or almond extract
- 1½ cups whole-wheat flour
- 1 cup unbleached or all-purpose flour
- 2 cups finely chopped walnuts
- 1 teaspoon baking soda
- ½ teaspoon salt
- 1½ cups semisweet chocolate chips

1. Preheat oven to 350°F and grease a baking sheet. Cream the butter in a large bowl with an electric mixer, slowly drizzling in the maple syrup. Dissolve the espresso powder in the hot water and beat that in, along with the vanilla.

2. In a separate bowl, toss the flours, walnuts, baking soda, and salt to mix. Stir into the creamed mixture, in several stages, until the flour is incorporated. Stir in the chocolate chips; don't beat the batter.

3. Let the batter sit for several minutes, then drop slightly mounded tablespoons of batter onto the baking sheet, leaving about 2 inches between the mounds. Bake for about 15 minutes — only one sheet at a time — just until the edges begin to brown. Transfer to a wire rack to cool.

Yield: About 2½ dozen

> After being cooped up inside all winter, [I] still love to sit out under the stars at night listening to the crackling of the wood burning under the pan, and watching the flames lick the sides of the smokestack.
>
> — Jeff Mitchell, sugarmaker

THE REAL THING: BUTTER

When it comes to cooking, maple syrup is not the only real thing that matters. I use real butter — unsalted — because it gives me more control over the final flavor of a dish. If you use salted butter, reduce the salt called for in the dish or in whatever you're baking (there's about ⅜ teaspoon of salt in a stick of butter).

MAPLE-SPICE COOKIES

Simple but special, these cookies were created by Sue Clark of Wells, Vermont, who has won many maple cooking and baking contests. George Cook, maple specialist at the University of Vermont Extension, says Sue and her husband, Bill, are "truly a maple couple." Bill's sugarmaking story is on the next page.

- 1 **cup vegetable shortening**
- 1 **cup firmly packed brown sugar**
- ½ **cup granulated sugar**
- ½ **cup dark (Grade B) maple syrup**
- 2 **eggs**
- 4 **cups unbleached or all-purpose flour**
- 2¼ **teaspoons baking soda**
- 2 **teaspoons ground ginger**
- 1½ **teaspoons ground cinnamon**
- ¼ **teaspoon salt**
  Granulated sugar

1. Preheat oven to 350°F. Grease a baking sheet. Cream the shortening, brown sugar, and granulated sugar in a large bowl until fluffy. Beat in the maple syrup and eggs, one at a time.

2. Combine the flour, baking soda, ginger, cinnamon, and salt in a medium-sized bowl. Add the flour mixture to the shortening mixture, a little at a time, and mix until well blended. The dough will be sticky.

3. Sprinkle granulated sugar onto a sheet of wax paper. Roll the dough into 1½-inch balls and dip the tops into the sugar. Place the balls 2 inches apart on the baking sheet.

4. Bake for 12 to 13 minutes, or until light golden brown and the center is set; do not overbake. Let cool on baking sheet for 1 minute. Transfer to a wire rack to cool completely.

Yield: 4 dozen cookies

Bill Clark

Bill Clark is responsible, not once but twice, for a renewed interest in maple-syrup. Back in the 1800s, just about every farm in Vermont had a maple orchard, and the Clark farm in Wells was no exception. But Bill's great-grandfather sold the maple lumber in 1893 to buy spruce lumber for a new barn. By the time Bill was 12 and his brother 10 years old, "there was a good maple orchard again." Fortuitously, school was shut down for a few weeks in what was called a "mud vacation." Bill and his brother went to the woods with 85 taps and made 15 gallons of syrup. Thus began the first maple renaissance.

In 1961, at a time when Bill says "the maple industry was going downhill in Vermont," he was "surprisingly" elected president of the Rutland County Maple Producers Association. Forty years and five days later he retired after 32 years as president of the Vermont Maple Sugar Makers' Association. "And sugaring is alive and well and a thriving industry today," Bill exclaims.

Bill and his wife, Sue, whose four kids "put in their hours and their days," have scaled back production on their farm. "After hosting 40,000 visitors from six continents over the years, I've reached the age where I don't need all that entertainment," Bill said, recalling the tourists who crowded the farm to watch him in the sugarhouse and who bought maple products and Sue's jams and jellies, as well as the years traveling the farmers' market circuit and serving the maple industry.

Bill's service has been well recognized. He's a member of the Maple Hall of Fame at the American Maple Museum in Croghan, New York, and the Vermont Legislature honored him as "Vermont's very special Mr. Maple" when he retired from the association. But he surely has not quit sugarmaking: Bill's Grade A Medium Amber syrup won the Best of Show award at the 2001 Vermont Farm Show.

MAPLE PUMPKIN COOKIES

Here's a soft, rather unusual cookie, packed with autumn highlights and a whisper of spice. The cookies have a light, cakey texture, so you can easily pack away 5 or 6 at a sitting. Great with cider or a cold glass of milk.

- 1 cup maple syrup
- 1 cup pumpkin purée, canned or freshly cooked and cooled
- 1 egg
- 1 teaspoon vanilla extract
- ½ cup (1 stick) butter, softened
- 1 cup unbleached or all-purpose flour
- 1 cup whole-wheat flour
- 1 teaspoon baking powder
- 1 teaspoon baking soda
- ½ teaspoon cinnamon
- ½ teaspoon nutmeg
- ½ teaspoon salt
- ½ cup chopped pecans
- 1 cup peeled, grated apple

1. Preheat oven to 350°F. Grease a baking sheet. Combine the maple syrup, pumpkin purée, egg, and vanilla in a food processor and process until smooth. Cream the butter with an electric mixer, then stir in about half of the pumpkin mixture.

2. In a separate bowl, toss together the flours, baking powder, baking soda, cinnamon, nutmeg, and salt.

3. Add the flour mixture and the pumpkin mixture alternately to the butter mixture, stirring after each addition just until blended. Fold in the pecans and apple.

4. Spoon heaping tablespoons of the batter, 2 inches apart, onto the prepared baking sheet. Bake for 15 to 20 minutes, until the bottom edges just start to brown. Transfer to racks and cool. Repeat with remaining batter.

Yield: About 3 dozen

BLONDE GINGER CUTOUT COOKIES

These are a lot like gingerbread cookies. They're my kids' favorite cookie to make, and they cut them into all sorts of shapes. It's important to chill the dough for at least 2 hours before you roll it, otherwise it will be difficult to handle.

- ⅔ cup vegetable shortening
- ⅓ cup (5⅓ tablespoons) butter, softened
- 1 cup pure maple syrup, at room temperature
- 1 tablespoon blackstrap molasses
- ½ teaspoon pure vanilla extract
- 4 cups unbleached or whole-wheat flour
- 2 teaspoons baking soda
- ½ teaspoon salt
- ½ teaspoon ginger
- ¼ teaspoon ground cloves
- ¼ teaspoon nutmeg

1. Cream together the shortening and butter in a large bowl. Gradually beat in the maple syrup, molasses, and vanilla. Mix the flour, baking soda, salt, ginger, cloves, and nutmeg and work them into the creamed mixture about 1 cup at a time. Using floured hands, divide the dough in half and wrap each half in plastic, each flattened into a disk. Chill for at least 2 hours.

2. Preheat oven to 350°F and lightly grease a baking sheet. Roll the dough out, one part at a time, onto a sheet of wax paper; make it a little less than ¼-inch thick. Cut into whatever shapes you like, transfer to the baking sheet, and bake for 10 to 12 minutes, until the bottoms are golden. Cool briefly on the sheet, then transfer to a wire rack to finish cooling.

Yield: Varies

FRUIT CRISP

This is a quick dessert to put together, especially if you've made a double batch of Oat-Crumb Topping and stashed some in the freezer. Simply slice fresh fruit, just about anything in season, to fill an 8-inch square pan. I'm partial to apple, pear, peach, berry, rhubarb, or some creative combination of the above, in my crisps.

Sprinkle the fruit with lemon juice or a touch of maple syrup, if desired, then spread the topping evenly over all. Bake at 350°F for 30 to 40 minutes, or until bubbly.

OAT-CRUMB TOPPING

A good, general-purpose crunchy topping for pies, bars, crumbles, crisps, and all those wonderful sweet things, this can be made with granulated or brown sugar. The disadvantage to the granulated sugar is that it tends to brown more quickly. But you can prevent excessive browning by loosely covering with foil.

½ cup unbleached or all-purpose flour
½ cup granulated or firmly packed brown sugar
⅓ cup old-fashioned oats
    Pinch of salt
    Pinch of ground cinnamon or more to taste
4 tablespoons cold butter, cut into ¼-inch pieces

1. Toss the flour, sugar, oats, salt, and cinnamon to mix in a large bowl.

2. Cut the butter into the flour mixture until the mixture is uniform and somewhat gravelly in texture. It shouldn't get to the point where it starts to clump together; stop if that happens. Refrigerate, covered, until you are ready to use. Freeze for longer storage.

Yield: About 1½ cups (enough for 1 pie or crisp)

Maggie Brox

Maggie Brox started sugaring in the mid-seventies. She and her then-husband put out some taps on borrowed land in Rumney, New Hampshire, collecting sap in a gathering tank attached to a dozer. Today she has around 1,600 taps on her own sugarbush, which in a good year yields about 350 gallons of syrup. I caught up with her when the 2001 syrup season was just winding down.

K: People have an idealized image of sugaring, like the scene on syrup cans — kids emptying sap buckets into gathering tanks on horse-drawn sleds — that sort of thing. Tell me a little about the reality.

M: Well, almost no one uses buckets anymore, except the hobbyists. Some producers hang a few buckets around the sugarhouse, for show, but everyone uses tubing these days. Gravity carries the sap from the trees right to the sugarhouse.

K: Any problems with the tubing?

M: Oh, yeah. The moose walk right though it and tear it down. Squirrels and bears like to chew on it. So it has to be repaired periodically. And cleaned.

K: What misconceptions do people have about maple syrup?

M: They don't realize just how much sap it takes to make a gallon of syrup. Or that it's made from sap at all. They think it comes out of the tree as syrup and we just put it in cans. And I've had people tell me they thought all maple syrup came from Vermont.

K: After all these years, can you predict when the sap is going to run?

M: Not always. It's supposed to run when you have warm days and cold nights, but I've had days like that where I got nothing at all. And I've seen it run when it's 33°F and snowing like mad. I've decided sap pretty much runs when it pleases.

CANDY MOLDS

There are many choices for candy molds. Rubber molds work best for maple syrup candy, but lightly greased metal and wood molds also work well. Even small disposable aluminum foil pans, lightly greased, can be used. Candy molds may be purchased at many craft stores, some department stores, and from specialty kitchen shops, catalogs, or Web sites.

MAPLE SYRUP CANDIES

If you crave the sweet maple candies sold at tourist shops, you need not wait until your next vacation to enjoy them. Maple syrup producers associations are eager to share these treats, and how to make them at home, to spread the gospel of pure maple syrup. This recipe is from the Vermont Maple Sugar Makers' Association/Vermont Maple Promotion Board; the Massachusetts Maple Producers have produced a helpful video about making maple cream and maple candy. If you haven't tried these maple candies, be forewarned: They're like no other treat you've ever experienced.

> 2 **cups pure light-grade maple syrup (Light Amber, U.S.; No. 1 Extra Light, Canada)**
> **A few drops of vegetable oil or butter**

1. Fill a large pot partially with water. Bring to a boil, and note the temperature of the boiling water with a candy thermometer. (Since water boils at different temperatures in different locations, it is important to follow this step.) Set some candy molds into a jelly-roll pan. Set aside. (If using metal or wood molds, lightly grease them.)

2. Empty the large pot and place the syrup in it. Add a few drops of oil. (Boiling maple syrup will foam up; the oil keeps the foam down. Buttering the rim of the pot will also help.)

3. Boil carefully over high heat without stirring, until the temperature of the boiling syrup is 28°F above the boiling point of water (212°F at sea level).

4. Remove from the heat, and let cool for 3 to 5 minutes. Do not stir or disturb the candy at this point; if the thermometer is attached to the pan, leave it during the cooling period.

5. Stir evenly until the liquid loses its gloss, starts to become opaque, and begins to thicken. (This is the tricky part; if you stir too long the thickened syrup will "set up," or harden, in the pan. If this happens, add a cup of water, and reheat slowly to dissolve the sugar, then start over. If you don't stir long enough, the sugar may not "set up" in the molds at all.)

6. Carefully pour the candy into the molds. It's helpful to have an assistant spread the syrup in the molds while you continue to pour the mixture into the other molds.

7. Allow the candies to cool, remove from molds, place on a rack to dry for a few hours, and enjoy.

Yield: 1 pound of candy

MAPLE FUDGE

A specialty of sugarhouses and tourist shops all over maple country, Maple Fudge is delicious but requires a good sense of timing. If you don't work quickly enough, you could be eating it out of the pan.

> 2 **cups granulated sugar**
> 1 **cup pure maple syrup, preferably Grade A Light Amber or No. 1 Extra Light**
> ½ **cup light cream**
> 2 **tablespoons butter**

1. Grease well an 8-inch-square pan. Combine all ingredients in a medium saucepan. Cook, stirring, over medium-high heat, until boiling.

2. Clip a candy thermometer to the side of the pan and continue cooking and stirring until the mixture reaches 238°F, about 10 to 15 minutes. Remove from heat and cool without stirring until lukewarm (110°F), about 1 hour.

3. Remove the candy thermometer and beat the mixture with a wooden spoon until the color lightens, the mixture loses its gloss, and the fudge begins to set. Quickly press into the prepared pan; score into squares while warm. When the fudge is firm, cut into squares. Store tightly covered.

Yield: 24 pieces

CANDIED POPCORN AND NUTS

My generation grew up on a mass-market version of this, and frankly I don't remember if it was the sweet popcorn or the prize at the bottom of the box we liked more. This maple version makes a special Christmas gift when packed into festive bags. Try to enlist the help of a second person to support the pot while you scrape the boiled liquid into the popcorn mix.

- 2 cups walnuts or other nutmeats
- 1 cup raw (untoasted) sunflower seeds
- 2 quarts popped popcorn, unsalted and unbuttered
- 1½ cups sugar
- ¾ cup pure maple syrup
- ½ cup water
- 4 tablespoons butter
- ½ teaspoon salt
- 1 teaspoon ground cinnamon
- 1 teaspoon pure vanilla extract

1. You will need three baking sheets for this; grease two of them very lightly and set aside. Preheat oven to 350°F.

2. Spread the nuts and seeds on the third baking sheet. In the preheated oven, toast the nuts and seeds for 7 minutes, stirring once. Turn off the oven. Remove the baking sheet; spread the popcorn on top of the nuts and seeds. Return to the oven to keep warm.

3. Bring the sugar, maple syrup, water, butter, and salt to a boil in a heavy-bottomed pot. Boil, partially covered, until the mixture reaches 290°F on a candy thermometer. Remove from the heat and then stir in the cinnamon and vanilla.

4. Quickly transfer the popcorn mix to the largest bowl you have and pour in the hot liquid. Working quickly — it will soon stiffen — stir to coat the entire mixture. Spread on the greased baking sheets and cool for 30 minutes. Break the mixture apart; store in plastic bags or tins.

Yield: About 2½ quarts

Maple Apple Pie

This is your basic maple apple pie with a small twist of lime, just enough to complement the maple flavor. It's a very full pie and it needs to bake a long time; don't be tempted to pull it out of the oven until the juices bubble thickly. You may substitute lemon for the lime if you'd like.

½   recipe Flaky Butter Crust (page 116) or other pie dough
8   cups peeled, cored, and thinly sliced cooking apples (about 6 large ones)
½   cup pure maple syrup
1½ tablespoons cornstarch
½   teaspoon finely grated lime zest
    Juice of ½ lime (about 1 tablespoon)
2   tablespoons butter cut into bits
1   recipe Oat-Crumb Topping (page 106)

1. Prepare the pastry and line a 9-inch pie plate with it. Form a decorative raised edge and freeze. Preheat oven to 425°F.

2. Put the sliced apples in a large bowl and pour on the maple syrup. Stir to coat the slices. Sift the cornstarch over the apples, stirring as you do so. Mix in the lime zest and juice. Turn the apples into the chilled crust and pat with your hands into an even mound. Dot with the butter. Cover the pie with loosely tented foil. Place the pie on a baking sheet and bake, on the center rack, for 20 minutes. Reduce oven to 375°F and cook for 10 minutes longer.

3. After the 10 minutes, remove the foil cover and evenly distribute the Oat-Crumb Topping over the top. Bake for another 45 to 60 minutes, until the juices bubble out thickly. If the top starts to get too dark, cover loosely with the foil. Cool on a rack.

Yield: 8–10 servings

Shaker Boiled Cider Pie

Boiled cider is little known today, but this pie is so good it may spark a revival. The pie filling is like a rich maple-apple custard with a very thin layer of meringue on top. Possibly my favorite pie to date.

½	recipe Flaky Butter Crust (page 116) or other pie dough
¾	cup boiled cider
¾	cup pure maple syrup
2	tablespoons butter
	Pinch of salt
3	eggs, separated and at room temperature
⅛	teaspoon nutmeg

1. Prepare the pastry according to the directions and line a 9-inch pie plate with the pastry. Form a slightly raised edge and freeze. Preheat oven to 350°F.

2. Gently warm the boiled cider, maple syrup, and butter in a small saucepan, just until the butter melts. Transfer to a large bowl and cool slightly. Whisk in the salt and egg yolks.

3. Beat the egg whites until stiff peaks form, then quickly whisk them into the cider mixture.

4. Pour the filling into the chilled crust and bake, on the center rack, for about 40 minutes. When done, the top will be dark brown and the pie will wobble just slightly, not in waves. Cool on a rack, dusting the surface with the nutmeg. Serve slightly warm or refrigerate and serve cold, which is the way I like it best. Great with vanilla ice cream or whipped cream.

Note: If you cover this pie, form a foil "tent" that doesn't touch the pie, or it will stick to the delicate meringue.

Yield: 8–10 servings

Maple Pecan Pie

Sweet, rich, and unabashedly decadent, this should be the standard against which all pecan pies are measured.

½   recipe Flaky Butter Crust (page 116) or
      other pie dough
3   eggs, at room temperature
1   cup pure maple syrup, at room temperature
½   cup firmly packed brown sugar
      Pinch of salt
1   teaspoon pure vanilla extract
1   tablespoon flour
1⅔ cups pecan halves

1. Prepare the pie shell according to the directions, line a 9-inch pie plate with the pastry, and refrigerate. Preheat oven to 425°F.

2. Using an electric mixer, beat the eggs on high speed for 2 minutes. Add the maple syrup, brown sugar, salt, vanilla, and flour and beat for another minute. Spread the pecans in the pie shell, then slowly pour in the egg mixture.

3. Bake on the center rack of the oven for 10 minutes, reduce oven to 375°F, then bake for about another 30 minutes. When done, the pie will be golden, puffed, and not soupy in the middle. Cool on a rack before slicing. Serve with vanilla ice cream.

Yield: 8–10 servings

Using Maple Sugar

Maple sugar, the sweetening staple of Native American and colonial diets, is sold in brick form and as granules, and may be purchased by mail or Internet order from maple producers.

It can be substituted in most recipes that call for granulated white or brown sugar. But the maple sugar granules are larger than refined sugar, which sometimes causes cakes to crack. If you want to use maple sugar in a cake, grind the sugar into smaller granules in a food processor.

French Canadian Maple Sugar Pie

Another recipe from my late friend Richard Sax, who credited it to a Quebec cousin-of-a-friend. He described this, quite aptly, as something like pecan pie with a nice tart edge. It's really excellent with vanilla ice cream. Where the recipe calls for brewed tea, I like lemon herbal tea.

½ **recipe Flaky Butter Crust (page 116) or other pie dough**

3 **eggs**

¾ **cup plus 2 tablespoons firmly packed brown sugar**

¾ **cup pure maple syrup**

6 **tablespoons butter, melted**

¼ **cup brewed tea**

2 **tablespoons plus ½ teaspoon apple cider vinegar**

Pinch of salt

¾ **cup coarsely chopped walnuts**

1. Prepare the pie shell according to the directions, line a 9-inch pie plate with the pastry, and refrigerate or freeze. Preheat oven to 450°F.

2. Whisk together the eggs and sugar in a large bowl. Add the maple syrup, butter, tea, vinegar, and salt, whisking until smooth. Stir in the walnuts. Place the pie shell on a heavy baking sheet and pour in the filling.

3. Place on the center rack of the oven and bake for 10 minutes. Then reduce oven to 350°F and continue to bake until the center is set, about 25 minutes longer. Cool on a wire rack. Serve warm or at room temperature. This is good cold, too.

Yield: 8–10 servings

SWEET POTATO PIE

Instead of the sweet potato purée, you could use an equal amount of winter squash, or even canned cold-pack pumpkin. This is easy and there's very little cleanup because the whole thing is mixed right in a food processor.

½ recipe Flaky Butter Crust (page 116), partially
   baked and cooled (step 9, page 117)
2 cups sweet potato purée (bake potatoes,
   then purée flesh)
3 eggs, at room temperature
½ cup pure maple syrup, at room temperature
1 cup light cream
1 tablespoon blackstrap molasses
1 teaspoon ground cinnamon
1 teaspoon ground allspice
1 teaspoon ground ginger
¼ teaspoon salt

1. Prepare the pie shell, line a 9-inch pie plate with the pastry, and refrigerate. Preheat oven to 425°F. Combine the filling ingredients in a food processor or blender and purée until smooth. Pour into the pie shell and bake on the center rack of the oven for 15 minutes.

2. Reduce oven to 350°F and bake for another 30 minutes, until a sharp knife inserted in the center of the pie comes out clean. Don't worry if the surface of the pie develops a crack; that's fine. Cool on a wire rack. Serve warm, at room temperature, or chilled.

Yield: 8–10 servings

POWDERED MAPLE

Just as technology has improved the efficiency of sugaring, it also has produced a method to dehydrate maple syrup into a powder. Reconstituting it takes only minutes; the powder is available by mail order.

FLAKY BUTTER CRUST

Everybody has their own special recipe for piecrust; this is one of mine. Made with both butter and a little vegetable shortening, it is flavorful and flaky. The little bit of lemon juice tenderizes the crust, so it's noticeably delicate. If you are using this for a top and bottom crust, make one half slightly larger than the other. Because so many of the pies in this book go from freezer to oven, it is important to use a metal or Pyrex pie plate.

2½ cups unbleached or all-purpose flour
½ teaspoon salt
¾ cup (1½ sticks) cold butter, cut into ¼-inch pieces
¼ cup vegetable shortening
1 tablespoon sugar
1 egg, cold
2 tablespoons ice water
1 tablespoon lemon juice or vinegar

1. Combine the flour and salt in a large bowl and toss to mix. Cut the butter and vegetable shortening into the flour until the butter is evenly distributed, with pieces of fat no larger than split peas. Add the sugar and toss with your fingers to incorporate.

2. Beat the egg, water, and lemon juice with a fork in a separate bowl. Drizzle half of this liquid over the flour, tossing the mixture with a fork. Add the rest of the liquid, tossing and blending as you pour. Work the mixture briefly with your fork, then try to pack the dough together, like a snowball. If dry spots remain, use wet fingertips to pull them into the ball of dough.

3. Divide the dough in half and flatten each half into a disk about ½-inch thick. Wrap each half in plastic and refrigerate for at least 30 minutes.

4. To roll the dough, place a 12-inch square piece of wax paper or plastic wrap on a work surface. Place half of the dough on it and roll the disk into a 12-inch circle. Dust the dough's surface with a little flour, if needed, to prevent the dough from sticking to your pin.

5. Flip the wax paper over, inverting the rolled dough over the pie plate, then peel off the paper. Tuck the dough into the pan, without stretching it.

6. IF YOU ARE MAKING A PIE SHELL: Trim the overhang to an even ½ inch, then tuck the overhang under, sculpting the edge into an upstanding ridge. Form a decorative edge, if desired, cover with plastic, and freeze.

7. IF YOU ARE MAKING A DOUBLE-CRUSTED PIE: Roll out half as for a pie shell, but do not trim. Cover with plastic, and refrigerate while you roll the top crust.

8. Fill the pie, run a moistened fingertip around the rim of the bottom crust and lay the top sheet of dough over the filling. Press down slightly where you've moistened the edge, to seal. Trim the overhang to an even ½ inch, then tuck it under, sculpting the edge into an upstanding ridge. Form a decorative edge, if desired, and poke three or four steam vents in the top crust with the tines of a fork. Bake as directed.

9. TO PARTIALLY PREBAKE A PIECRUST: Preheat oven to 425°F. Line the frozen shell with a 12-inch square of foil, tucking it into the contours of the pan. Spread about 2 cups of dried rice or beans in the bottom and slightly up the sides of the foil. Bake the crust in the lower part of the oven for 15 minutes, then carefully lift out the foil and beans. Prick the bottom several times with a fork, so steam can escape. Reduce oven to 375°F and bake for another 10 minutes. Cool on a wire rack.

10. TO FULLY PREBAKE A PIE SHELL: Proceed as above, but bake the crust for about 20 minutes after lowering the heat, until evenly browned.

Yield: One double-crusted 9-inch pie or two 9-inch pie shells

Simple Rhubarb Pie

Originally, I went through all sorts of convulsions trying to make this an "interesting" pie. I added strawberries, cherries, and on and on, because I was afraid rhubarb would live up to its reputation as something of a culinary wallflower. Each time, the pie was great, but the subtle rhubarb and maple flavors were being crowded out by my tampering. When I finally woke up and kept just rhubarb and maple, I knew I'd hit the mark. Strike one for simplicity.

½ recipe Flaky Butter Crust (page 116) or
    other pie dough
5 cups sliced rhubarb (½-inch pieces)
¼ cup sugar
⅔ cup pure maple syrup
1 teaspoon vanilla extract
¼ cup unbleached or all-purpose flour
    Oat-Crumb Topping (page 106)

1. Prepare the pie shell according to the directions, line a 9-inch pie plate with the pastry, and refrigerate or freeze. Preheat the oven to 400°F.

2. Combine the rhubarb with the sugar. Stir, then set aside for 15 minutes. Stir in the maple syrup, vanilla, and flour.

3. Turn the filling into the chilled pie shell and even out the top. Bake on the lower rack for 20 minutes.

4. Remove the pie from the oven, reduce the heat to 375°F, and place the pie on a baking sheet with sides (to catch the juices). Spread the topping evenly over the pie and return it to the oven, on the middle rack. Bake for another 40 to 50 minutes until the juices bubble thickly. Cool on a rack. Slice and serve when slightly warm.

Yield: 8–10 servings

UPSIDE-DOWN SKILLET PEAR TART

This rustic tart, baked in a cast-iron skillet, is sublime. This is just the tart to bring along to a fall potluck or party.

½	recipe Flaky Butter Crust (page 116) or other pie dough
2	tablespoons butter
⅓	cup pure maple syrup
2	tablespoons sugar
6	large pears, halved, cored, and peeled

1. Prepare the pastry according to the directions through step 3, page 116, and refrigerate. Preheat oven to 400°F.

2. Melt the butter in a medium cast-iron skillet. Stir in the maple syrup and sugar and bring to a low boil, stirring. Boil for 1½ minutes, then remove from the heat.

3. Arrange the pears in the skillet, rounded side down and points toward the center. Put two halves in the center, pointed in opposite directions. Any remaining halves can be sliced and interspersed on top of the others. Try to keep the top level of the pears even, but don't lose any sleep over it — it's bound to be jagged.

4. Roll the pastry into a 12-inch circle. Lay it on top of the pears and tuck the edge down between the pears and the side of the skillet. Make two or three wide slashes in the crust, so steam can escape. Bake for 45 minutes.

5. Remove the tart from the oven and let cool for 10 minutes.

6. Place a plate directly on top of the crust. Ideally, it should just fit the skillet. Quickly invert the tart, tilting it slightly away from you to avoid getting hot syrup on your hands and arms. (This is best done over a sink.) Let cool at least 15 minutes before cutting. It will probably be a little juicy; that's fine. Any juice can be spooned over the pears to glaze them.

Yield: 8 servings

Buttermilk Maple Spice Cake

In general, I like to make simple cakes, such as this one. The spices can be increased, but don't go too heavy on the spice or you'll mask the subtle maple flavor. A good snack item for brown baggers or for dessert, with whipped cream.

- 1 cup unbleached or all-purpose flour
- ½ cup whole-wheat flour
- 1 teaspoon baking powder
- 1 teaspoon baking soda
- ½ teaspoon ground cinnamon
- ½ teaspoon ground ginger
- ½ teaspoon salt
- ¼ teaspoon ground cloves
- ¼ teaspoon ground nutmeg
   Pinch of cayenne
- 2 eggs, lightly beaten
- ⅔ cup buttermilk
- ½ cup pure maple syrup
- ⅓ cup vegetable oil
- 1 tablespoon blackstrap molasses

1. Preheat oven to 350°F. Grease a 9-inch square baking pan.

2. Sift the flours, baking powder, baking soda, cinnamon, ginger, salt, cloves, nutmeg, and cayenne into a large bowl. Set aside.

3. In another bowl, blend the eggs, buttermilk, maple syrup, oil, and molasses.

4. Make a well in the dry mixture and stir in the egg mixture, just until smooth; do not beat. Pour the batter into the prepared pan and bake for 30 minutes, until a tester inserted into the center comes out clean. Cool in the pan.

Yield: 9–12 servings

TAWNY MAPLE CHEESECAKE

Having spent a fair chunk of my youth cruising the New Jersey diner circuit, I know a thing or two about cheesecakes. I know, for instance, that I like mine light, moist, and creamy — and hold the canned fruit toppings please. That's why I like this one. This is wonderful with a cup of coffee, about an hour after dinner (or before breakfast).

1¼	cups fine graham cracker crumbs
5	tablespoons sugar
5	tablespoons butter, softened
¾	cup pure maple syrup
¼	cup cold heavy cream
24	ounces (three 8-ounce packages) cream cheese, softened
3	eggs, at room temperature
1½	cups sour cream, at room temperature
1½	teaspoons pure vanilla extract

1. Combine the cracker crumbs and 1 tablespoon of the sugar in a small bowl with the soft butter. Combine thoroughly, then press into the bottom of a 9-inch springform pan. Freeze. Preheat oven to 350°F.

2. Bring the maple syrup to a boil in a medium-sized saucepan over medium heat. Boil for 3 minutes, remove from the heat, and stir in the cream. Scrape into a bowl and refrigerate.

3. Using a heavy-duty electric mixer, cream the cream cheese until light and fluffy. Add the remaining 4 tablespoons sugar and beat briefly, then add the eggs, one at a time, incorporating after each addition. When the maple syrup is no longer warm to the touch, gradually beat it in, followed by the sour cream and vanilla.

4. Scrape into the chilled pan and bake for 1 hour. Carefully transfer to a wire rack and cool thoroughly. Cover, then chill for at least 6 hours before serving.

Yield: 16 servings

[Maple syrup] is readily and economically produced, almost rivaling the snow in whiteness and purity, pleasant to the sight, and exceedingly pleasant to the taste.

— S. Scudder, in a Letter to the Editor of *American Agriculturist*, February 1858

CARROT CAKE

When my friends Mike and Nancy got married, I multiplied this recipe by about a zillion and made it into a multitiered wedding cake for two hundred. And they all liked it. I think this cake gets its special character and appeal from the maple, whole-wheat flour, and ground almonds.

CAKE

4	eggs
1	cup pure maple syrup, at room temperature
1¼	cups light vegetable oil
½	cup sour cream
1	tablespoon lemon juice
1	teaspoon pure vanilla extract
1	teaspoon almond extract
1	cup whole-wheat flour
1	cup unbleached or all-purpose flour
1½	cups finely ground almonds (almost the consistency of almond meal; use a food processor)
1	tablespoon baking powder
1	teaspoon ground allspice
1	teaspoon ground cinnamon
½	teaspoon salt
	Finely grated zest of 1 orange
2	cups grated carrots (about ¾ pound carrots)
1	cup raisins

FROSTING

12	ounces cream cheese, softened
⅔	cup pure maple syrup, at room temperature
1	teaspoon pure vanilla extract
1	teaspoon finely grated lemon zest

1. Preheat oven to 350°F. Grease a 9- by 13-inch baking pan.

2. Using an electric mixer, beat the eggs on high speed for 1 minute. Continue to beat, gradually adding the maple syrup, oil, sour cream, lemon juice, and vanilla and almond extracts.

3. In a separate bowl, sift together the whole-wheat and unbleached flours. Then stir in the almonds, baking powder, allspice, cinnamon, salt, and orange zest.

4. Make a well in the dry ingredients, then add the liquids all at once. Stir just until smooth, then fold in the carrots and raisins. Scrape into the prepared pan and bake for 35 to 40 minutes, until a tester inserted into the center comes out clean. Cool in the pan, on a wire rack, then frost.

5. **To make the frosting:** Beat the cream cheese with an electric mixer until soft and fluffy. Gradually add the maple syrup, vanilla, and lemon zest. Ice the cake when it has cooled.

Yield: 12–15 servings

Maple Butter Frosting

For a rich finishing touch for the Maple Cranberry-Nut Coffee Cake (page 38) or Buttermilk Maple Spice Cake (page 120), this easy recipe from Jo Burnett of Burnett's Maple Farm in Conway, Massachusetts, can't be beat.

- ½ **cup (1 stick) butter, softened**
- 3 **cups confectioners' sugar**
- 4–6 **tablespoons pure maple syrup**
- ¼ **cup chopped walnuts or pecans**

1. Using an electric mixer, thoroughly cream together the butter and sugar, then gradually add the maple syrup until the frosting is light and spreadable.

2. Stir in the nuts.

Yield: 1¾ cups (enough for a 9-inch layer cake)

Maple Mocha Pudding

Classic comfort food, this, the sort of thing we all cherished as kids and now secretly yearn for since the onset of rampant mousse-ification. You get a rich maple flavor here, intensified by the coffee and cocoa — a winning team effort. I ladle this into small glass dessert bowls or goblets and serve with plenty of whipped cream.

- 3 tablespoons cornstarch
- 1 tablespoon powdered instant coffee or powdered instant espresso
- 1 teaspoon unsweetened cocoa
- Pinch of salt
- 3 egg yolks
- 3 cups milk
- ½ cup pure maple syrup
- 1 tablespoon butter, cut into pieces
- 1 teaspoon pure vanilla extract

1. Combine the cornstarch, coffee, cocoa, and salt in a large, heavy-bottomed pot and whisk to mix. Whisk the egg yolks slightly in a medium-sized bowl, then add the milk and maple syrup. Stir into the cornstarch mixture and begin to heat over medium-high heat.

2. Gradually bring the mixture to a boil, stirring gently but constantly. Be sure to scrape the sides as you stir. When the mixture finally comes to a boil, boil for 1 minute, stirring. Remove from the heat and stir in the butter and vanilla.

3. Ladle into four or five individual serving bowls. To prevent a skin from forming, place a piece of wax paper — cut to size — on top of each. Cool, then chill for several hours before serving.

Yield: 4–5 servings

INDIAN PUDDING

Indian pudding, from what I understand, is the oldest New England dessert on record. One taste of this soft, creamy maple version and you'll quickly understand why this dessert has a history behind it. A number of restaurants have built their reputations on their versions of Indian pudding, including the famous Durgin Park in Boston. I've had theirs; this one's better.

5	**cups milk**
⅔	**cup cornmeal**
1	**cup pure maple syrup**
1	**cup raisins or finely chopped dates**
4	**tablespoons butter**
1	**tablespoon blackstrap molasses**
½	**teaspoon ground cinnamon**
½	**teaspoon ground ginger**
½	**teaspoon salt**

1. Preheat oven to 300°F. Grease a shallow, 9- by 13-inch casserole dish.

2. Heat the milk in a large, heavy-bottomed pot over medium heat. Slowly sprinkle in the cornmeal, whisking as you do so. Switch to a wooden spoon and continue to cook and stir for about 10 minutes, until the mixture has thickened. Reduce the heat, add the maple syrup, raisins, butter, molasses, cinnamon, ginger, and salt, and stir for another minute or two. Pour into the prepared baking dish and bake for 2½ hours. Serve warm, with plenty of vanilla ice cream.

Yield: About 8 servings

SCALDING

To scald milk or cream, heat it to just below the boiling point, until tiny bubbles form around the edge of the pot. It helps to rinse the pan first in cold water, for easier cleanup. Milk or cream can also be scalded in the microwave oven if you have a temperature probe; set it for 180°F.

CRÈME BRÛLÉE

Crème Brûlée, the king of custards, has probably done more recently to broaden the waistlines of restaurant-goers in the United States than any other dessert. This version, though slightly less rich than most, is taking its toll on my own midregion. Begin this the day before you plan to serve it.

6	egg yolks
½	cup pure maple syrup
2	cups light cream
1	cup heavy cream
1	teaspoon vanilla extract
6	tablespoons light brown sugar

1. Preheat oven to 325°F. Bring about 4 cups of water to a boil and reserve.

2. *Very lightly* whisk the egg yolks and maple syrup together. Set aside. Scald (see Scalding) the light and heavy creams in a heavy-bottomed saucepan.

3. Gradually stir the hot cream into the yolk/maple syrup mixture, until blended. Do not beat it or the finished texture will be grainy. Stir in the vanilla. Ladle into six individual, ovenproof custard cups or ramekins of about ¾-cup capacity, filling almost to the rim.

4. Place the cups in a large, shallow casserole, then carefully pour in the boiled water until it reaches about halfway up the sides of the cups. Take care not to splash water into the cups. Cover loosely with foil, then bake for 1 hour, until a knife inserted near the center comes out clean. Cool to room temperature, cover with plastic, then refrigerate overnight.

5. About an hour before serving, remove the cups from the refrigerator. Sieve 1 tablespoon of brown sugar directly on top of each custard, spreading it evenly with a fork. Put the cups in a shallow casserole, then pour in enough ice water to come halfway up the sides of the cups. Turn on the broiler and broil the custard close to the heat, until the brown sugar bubbles and darkens; watch carefully, or it will burn. Cool and serve.

Yield: 6 servings

BAKED CUSTARD

Baked custard is one of the simplest things in the world to make, and a real crowd-pleaser when it is made with maple syrup. One thing to remember about custard is not to beat it excessively, which only makes the finished texture grainy. Just stir everything together nice and easy, then ladle into custard cups. I think the maple flavor comes out best when this is served cold, but warm custard has its proponents, too.

    4   eggs, lightly beaten
    ½   cup pure maple syrup
    1   teaspoon pure vanilla extract
    ¼   teaspoon salt
    3   cups milk, heated just to the boiling point

1. Preheat oven to 350°F. Bring about 4 cups of water to a boil and reserve.

2. With a whisk, gently blend the eggs, maple syrup, vanilla, and salt. Slowly stir in the hot milk. Ladle into six custard cups, filling each to within ¼ inch of the rim.

3. Place the cups in a large, shallow casserole dish and carefully pour the boiled water into the pan, until it comes about halfway up the cups. Bake for about 50 minutes, until a knife inserted near the center comes out clean. Serve warm, or cool to room temperature, cover, and chill.

Yield: 6 servings

MAPLE-GINGER ICE CREAM

I can hardly ever wait until this is completely frozen to savor a spoonful — or two. It has a lovely gingery flavor that does not overwhelm the maple, and it does not require an ice-cream maker. This is another recipe from the Citadelle Maple Producers' Cooperative in Canada. They sure know how to make it with maple up there.

- ¾ cup heavy cream
- 3 tablespoons pure maple syrup
- 1 cup light cream
- ½ cup milk
- ¼ cup confectioners' sugar
- 2 teaspoons pure vanilla extract
- 1 tablespoon ginger root, peeled and grated, or ¼ cup finely chopped crystallized ginger
- 2 teaspoons white rum, optional

1. Whisk the heavy cream and maple syrup until stiff. Set aside.

2. Heat the light cream, milk, sugar, and vanilla in a heavy saucepan over low heat, stirring continuously until sugar is dissolved, or about 1 minute. Fold in the heavy cream mixture.

3. Pour into a 2-quart container, cover, and freeze for approximately 2 hours, or until mushy.

4. Turn into a chilled bowl, beat with a whisk, and add the ginger and rum, if desired.

5. Return the container to the freezer and freeze until firm, about 4 hours. Serve with maple syrup.

Yield: 4–6 servings

Maple-Walnut Ice Cream

This is an excellent, basic maple ice cream, good alone or with cake or pie. One thing I love to do with this is to create the Ultimate Death by Chocolate Waffles Experience. You put down a waffle (page 20), mound it with this ice cream, then scoop on lots of fresh sliced strawberries. Besides being a pretty special breakfast, it might replace the cake at your next birthday party.

2	cups light cream
⅔	cup pure maple syrup
⅓	cup sugar
2	teaspoons pure vanilla extract
1½	cups heavy cream
½	cup milk
1	cup chopped walnuts
½	teaspoon ground cinnamon, optional

1. Gently heat 1 cup of the light cream, the maple syrup, and the sugar in a heavy saucepan, just until the sugar is dissolved. Remove from the heat and stir in the vanilla.

2. Pour into a shallow casserole dish and chill in the freezer until it is very cold. After it has thoroughly chilled, combine it with the remaining 1 cup light cream, heavy cream, and milk in the freezing can of an ice-cream maker. Process according to the manufacturer's directions.

3. When it reaches finished consistency, stir in the nuts and cinnamon, if desired. I like to let this firm up in the freezer for several hours, if possible, before eating it.

Yield: About 1 quart

BEVERAGE BOOSTER

Maple aficionados often use good-quality light maple syrup in drink recipes that call for simple syrup (or sugar syrup). It's easier than cooking the mixture of sugar and water needed for simple syrup. So think about maple in your coolers, daiquiris, sours, margaritas — and even lemonade.

ICED-MAPLE ESPRESSO SHAKE

If you love coffee and ice cream, this recipe alone may be grounds for leaving me in your will. It is simply addicting. On more than one hot summer's eve, I've been known to skip dinner in favor of a frosty mug of this. It couldn't be quicker to make — just buzz it all in the blender and serve. Refreshing!

  3 **ice cubes**
  ¾ **cup cold, brewed espresso or other strong coffee**
  ½ **cup milk**
  ¼ **cup pure maple syrup**
  ½ **pint good-quality vanilla ice cream**
  1 **tablespoon coffee liqueur, optional**

1. Chill two big glasses in the freezer. Put the ice cubes inside a folded tea towel and crush them, just a little, with a hammer.

2. Combine the crushed ice, espresso, milk, maple syrup, ice cream, and liqueur, if desired, in a blender. Process briefly until smooth, but with a slight slushy texture. Pour into the frosted mugs and enjoy.

Yield: 2 servings (or less, depending on your willpower)

Metric Conversions and U.S. Equivalents

Unless you have finely calibrated measuring equipment, conversions between U.S. and metric measurements will be somewhat inexact. It's important to convert the measurements for all of the ingredients in a recipe to maintain the same proportions as the original.

Approximate Metric Equivalents by Weight

U.S.	METRIC
¼ ounce	7 grams
½ ounce	14 grams
1 ounce	28 grams
1¼ ounces	35 grams
1½ ounces	40 grams
2½ ounces	70 grams
4 ounces	112 grams
5 ounces	140 grams
8 ounces	228 grams
10 ounces	280 grams
15 ounces	425 grams
16 ounces (1 pound)	454 grams

METRIC	U.S.
1 gram	0.035 ounce
50 grams	1.75 ounces
100 grams	3.5 ounces
250 grams	8.75 ounces
500 grams	1.1 pounds
1 kilogram	2.2 pounds

Approximate Metric Equivalents by Volume

U.S.	METRIC
1 teaspoon	5 milliliters
1 tablespoon	15 milliliters
¼ cup	60 milliliters
½ cup	120 milliliters
1 cup	230 milliliters
1¼ cups	300 milliliters
1½ cups	360 milliliters
2 cups	460 milliliters
2½ cups	600 milliliters
3 cups	700 milliliters
4 cups (1 quart)	0.95 liter
1.06 quarts	1 liter
4 quarts (1 gallon)	3.8 liters

General Formula for Metric Conversion

Ounces to grams	multiply ounces by 28.35
Grams to ounces	multiply grams by 0.035
Pounds to grams	multiply pounds by 453.5
Pounds to kilograms	multiply pounds by 0.45
Cups to liters	multiply cups by 0.24
Fahrenheit to Celsius	subtract 32 from Fahrenheit temperature, multiply by 5, then divide by 9
Celsius to Fahrenheit	multiply Celsius temperature by 9, divide by 5, then add 32

Maple Information and Sources

Producers & Organizations

For information about maple syrup production, local producers, or maple festivals, contact one of these organizations or your state or province's agriculture department.

Citadelle Maple Syrup Producers'
Cooperative (Quebec)
819-362-3241
www.citadelle-camp.com

Kortright Centre for Conservation
(Ontario)
416-661-6600
www.kortright.org

Maine Maple Producers Association
207-634-3521
www.mainemapleproducers.com

Massachusetts Maple Producers
Association
413-628-3912
www.massmaple.org

Michigan Maple Syrup Association
989-685-2807
www.mi-maplesyrup.com

New York State Maple Producers
Association
607-535-9790
www.nysmaple.com

Ontario Maple Syrup Producers
Association
519-674-4000
www.ontariomaple.com

Quebec Maple Syrup Producers'
Federation
450-679-7021
www.siropderable.ca

Vermont Maple Sugar Makers' Association
Vermont Maple Foundation
802-763-7435
www.vtmaple.org

Wisconsin Maple Syrup Producers
Association
715-447-5758
www.wismaple.org

Suppliers

Many of the organizations listed previously provide information about suppliers for maple products. The sources that follow offer specialty products used in recipes in this book.

Bob's Sugar House
Dover-Foxcroft, Maine
207-564-2145
www.mainemaplesyrup.com
Maple syrup, maple butter, maple cream, and maple jelly

Boyajian, Inc.
Canton, Massachusetts
800-965-0665
www.boyajianinc.com
Maple vinegar and other infused vinegars and oils.

Canadian Maple Delights
Vancouver, British Columbia
604-682-6175
www.mapledelights.com
Maple vinegar and other maple products.

DeLoughary's Sugar Bush
Bark River, Michigan
800-506-2753
www.maplecream.com
Maple syrup, maple cream, and maple mustard

MapleLand Farms
Salem, New York
518-854-7669
www.maplelandfarms.com
Maple mustard, maple syrup, and maple cream

Trask Maple Products
Rutland, Vermont
802-775-2445
http://traskmapleproducts.com
Maple syrup, maple butter, maple cream, and maple syrup

Wood's Cider Mill
Springfield, Vermont
802-263-5547
www.woodscidermill.com
Boiled cider, cider syrup, and maple syrup

Acknowledgments and Recipe Credits

Many individuals and organizations contributed to the revision of *Maple Syrup Cookbook*.

Acknowledgments

At the risk of forgetting someone (please forgive), particular thanks are owed to:

Richard Acheson of the Citadelle Maple Syrup Producers' Cooperative; sugarmakers Maggie Brox and Bill and Sue Clark; Angie Considine of the New England Agricultural Statistics Service; George L. Cook, maple specialist at the University of Vermont Extension Service; Jacquelin Coté of Agriculture and Agri-Food Canada; Wendy Heron of the Kortright Centre for Conservation; Bruce Martell of the Vermont Department of Agriculture; Tom McCrumm of the Massachusetts Maple Producers Association; and Kathleen Williams of Storey Books.

Recipe Credits

Recipe on page 92 printed by permission of Boyajian, Inc.

Recipe on page 123 courtesy of Jo Burnett, Burnett's Maple Farm, Conway, Massachusetts.

Recipes on pages 17, 34, 56, 57, 91, and 128 printed by permission of the Citadelle Maple Syrup Producers' Cooperative.

Recipe on page 102 courtesy of Bill and Sue Clark, Clark Farm, Wells, Vermont.

Recipe on page 84 reprinted from *Cooking in the Shaker Spirit* by James Haller and Jeffrey Paige, Yankee Books, 1990, printed by permission of James Haller and Jeffrey Paige, Three Hills Publishing, P.O. Box 110, South Berwick, Maine 03908.

Recipe on page 88 courtesy of the Kortright Centre for Conservation.

Recipes on pages 49 and 69 courtesy of the Maine Maple Producers Association.

Recipe on page 82 courtesy of Tom McCrumm and Sue Haupt.

Recipe on page 65 printed by permission of the Ontario Maple Syrup Producers Association.

Recipe on page 40 courtesy of Bill Schneider, Browning Brook Maple, Colrain, Massachusetts.

Recipes on pages 96 and 108 printed by permission of The Vermont Maple Promotion Board.

Recipe on page 66 courtesy of Janice Wentworth, Warren Farm & Sugarhouse, North Brookfield, Massachusetts.

Index

Note: Page numbers in **boldface** refer to tables.

Other Storey Titles You Will Enjoy

250 Treasured Country Desserts, by Andrea Chesman & Fran Raboff.
A nostalgic collection of more than 250 recipes for home bakers
to rely on for all occasions.
416 pages. Paper. ISBN 978-1-60342-152-2.

Apple Cookbook, by Olwen Woodier.
More than 140 recipes to put everyone's favorite fruit
into tasty new combinations.
192 pages. Paper. ISBN 978-1-58017-389-6.

Maple Sugar, by Tim Herd.
From sap to syrup: the history, lore, and how-to
behind this sweet treat.
144 pages. Paper. ISBN 978-1-60342-735-7.

Recipes from the Root Cellar, by Andrea Chesman.
A collection of more than 250 recipes for winter kitchen
produce — jewel-toned root vegetables, hardy greens,
sweet winter squashes, and potatoes of every kind.
400 pages. Paper. ISBN 978-1-60342-545-2.

Serving Up the Harvest, by Andrea Chesman.
A collection of 175 recipes to bring out the best in garden-fresh
vegetables, with 14 master recipes that can accommodate
whatever happens to be in your produce basket.
512 pages. Paper. ISBN 978-1-58017-663-7.

These and other books from Storey Publishing are available
wherever quality books are sold or by calling 1-800-441-5700.
Visit us at *www.storey.com* or sign up for our newsletter
at *www.storey.com/signup.*